ENDORSEMENTS

Broken to Build masterfully delves into the divine process of experiencing brokenness in order to be rebuilt stronger in faith and character. Drawing from the author's journey, this transformative book serves as a beacon of hope, guiding readers to embrace their brokenness as a pathway to healing, wholeness, and accelerated spiritual growth in God.

Archbishop R. L. Dennis,
Kingdom Fellowship Covenant Ministries

The Greek word for equipping is *katartismos,* which means alignment. It is a medical term that refers to aligning a bone that was broken and setting it in place so it can heal. Therefore, when we talk about equipping the saints for the work of ministry, we are talking about aligning them for the work of ministry. Author and prophetic voice Crystal speaks directly to those who have been broken, misaligned, and "out of commission" in this book. The words of each chapter will ensure healing and proper alignment (or realignment) for every reader, allowing them to thrive in their God-given destiny and purpose.

Bishop Damien L. Sneed,
Ramah Gathering International Ministries

Broken to Build

I'm Breaking You Down To Build You Up

Crystal Love

EDITED BY

Nicole Queen

I dedicate this book to my parents, the late Prophet Jacob Schroeder and Missionary Exemea Schroeder. I am profoundly grateful to God for their unwavering love and dedication to serving in the Body of Christ. They devoted their lives to ensuring that my two older brothers and I were grounded in the teachings of Jesus Christ.

Their legacies continue to thrive through us as we embrace the spiritual mantles they have passed down. I often hear the echoes of their wisdom, which still resonate within me today, guiding me in living an effective life in Christ. I will always cherish the joyful memories of growing up in such a loving family, where faith was not just preached but lived out daily. The laughter, the lessons, and the countless moments of grace have shaped me into who I am today.

This book is a tribute to them and a reflection of the values they instilled in us, as we continue to build on the foundation they set in place.

CONTENTS

INTRODUCTION

Welcome to the transformative journey of being broken and rebuilt. Your past or current position and accomplishments hold little significance in this process. This should be considered because the brand new is packaged differently, and you can expect change. If you embrace it, you will witness a new version of yourself. The Lord has revealed to me that we should all remain in a state of brokenness before Him. By doing so, we will continually experience growth and supernatural endurance in our pursuit of God. There will never be a point where we do not see the fruit of God's work within us, as long as our hearts remain fertile and open for His guidance in planning, nurturing, and harvesting.

"I am the vine; you are the branches. If you remain in me and I in you, you will bear much fruit; apart from me, you can do nothing."

— JOHN 15:5

The Bible declares, "While the earth remains, seedtime and harvest, cold and heat, winter and summer, and day and night shall not cease" (Genesis 8:22). This reminds us that just as the seasons continue, our lives will go through different phases of growth and fulfillment. To live in God's perfect will for our lives, we must walk in total obedience to His plan, diligently following His instructions in His appointed time. This will lead us to a life of productivity and abundance, fulfilling the promises He has for us. This book was birthed out in and through my process of being broken and built into the new me. Have you ever prayed for change and known that it's on the horizon, but had no idea how it would happen? Sometimes transitions happen gradually, but other times they hit you with a powerful thrust, propelling you into your next position in life.

As I prepared two particular messages for two women's conferences in 2023, I had no idea that these messages would also speak directly to me. It was after delivering these messages to God's women that I found myself going through a process of being broken down so that God could rebuild me anew. He reminded me not to disregard everything that happened prior to this transformative experience but also assured me that I had reached the full capacity of all that had been planted, poured into, and nurtured within me in the past. Even the neglected parts were made to work for my good.

As I write this book and as you read it, I want you to know that it was a process that I have personally walked through and am walking through. While reading, I pray that God begins to speak to you about where you currently are and where you are headed. In the pages ahead, I want you to revisit your past, not with shame or guilt, but with a desire to fully allow God to heal the traumatic places in your life that you have not allowed Him to address. The Lord once revealed to me that healing is like undergoing anesthesia during surgery. Some aspects of the process occur unconsciously, behind the scenes. Throughout my journey with God, there have been times when I've only understood a portion of the process. I will delve deeper into this in a later chapter. God reveals information to us gradually, based on our maturity and capacity to comprehend.

At the age of 20, I yielded to the call of the Lord and entered ministry. That's when I preached my first sermon, based on the parable of the sower found in the book of Matthew, entitled "Too Much Is At Stake." Often, I would regret my progress, thinking I should be further along by now. However, the Lord had to teach me that the 24-year process I went through was necessary for my growth, learning, and experience. It also included moments that were prolonged and could have been avoided. This reminds me of the experiences of Moses and Joshua, of knowing what God promised but obtaining it only at the appointed time. Nevertheless, the Lord assured me that I have covered ground so that I can now assist others in saving time, heartache, and disappointment. Both individually and as a collective body within the body of Christ, we have certain processes we must go through. Some we will understand in this lifetime, while others will only be revealed in eternity when we are in our glorified bodies, experiencing the new heavens, the new earth, and the new Jerusalem.

GOD'S COMMAND

Being broken is part of the call of God that is on your life. It is where God is calling you from the place where you are to the place that He is revealing to you. Ultimately, a lot of people know what they have been purposed to do. Though you may not know all of the details, you have an idea of what your call is. As you are continuously obedient to what God shows you and what He tells you to do, He begins to reveal more and more. God is commanding you in this season to come out of your place of comfortability and complacency to a place that may feel awkward or strange, definitely unknown. But this move that you're getting ready to make in this season will not just change your life but all of those that are connected to your future, your now, and those that are coming after you. Being broken will cost you everything! The life that you once knew will be transformed into a life that you have not known yet.

> "The Lord had said to Abram, 'Go from your country, your people and your father's household to the land I will show you. I will make you into a great nation, and I will bless you; I will make your name great, and you will be a blessing. I will bless those who bless you, and whoever curses you I will curse; and all peoples on earth will be blessed through you."
>
> — GENESIS 12:1-3

Are you ready to leave it all for the next? Are you willing to sacrifice what you once knew as safe for something risky, unsure of what the outcome will be? With God, the creator of the universe, He is always our safe place, our stronghold.

"The Lord is a refuge for the oppressed, a stronghold in times of trouble."

— PSALM 9:9

So, get ready. As you turn each page of this book, something will be broken off of you, and something will be added to you. You will be transformed.

1. Don't Forget About Me
I'm Getting It All

This is the foundation from which we will start in the process of brokenness. As I delved deeper into this journey, I returned to the beginning and prayed, asking the Holy Spirit to reveal the true essence of brokenness and to help me explain it in simpler terms. I will approach this topic from different perspectives and angles throughout the book, but this is the foundational context from which I will be coming.

The Lord led me to Proverbs Chapter 15, and He said that this entire chapter has many vital viewpoints that guide you on how to remain broken before the Lord. This state of brokenness is a place of total surrender before Him, yielding yourself to His purpose for your life, and staying closely connected to Him, inclining your ear to His voice. This allows Him to bring healing and wholeness, and enables you to be an effective disciple in the world. When we yield ourselves completely to Him, it will cause the nations to come to Christ.

As you begin to read Proverbs 15, meditate on what each verse is saying, and you will see the outcomes of a person who is continuously broken before God compared to someone who is not.

Proverbs 15

¹ A gentle answer turns away wrath,
   but a harsh word stirs up anger.
² The tongue of the wise adorns knowledge,
   but the mouth of the fool gushes folly.
³ The eyes of the Lord are everywhere,
   keeping watch on the wicked and the good.
⁴ The soothing tongue is a tree of life,
   but a perverse tongue crushes the spirit.
⁵ A fool spurns a parent's discipline,
   but whoever heeds correction shows prudence.
⁶ The house of the righteous contains great treasure,
   but the income of the wicked brings ruin.
⁷ The lips of the wise spread knowledge,
   but the hearts of fools are not upright.
⁸ The Lord detests the sacrifice of the wicked,
   but the prayer of the upright pleases him.
⁹ The Lord detests the way of the wicked,
   but he loves those who pursue righteousness.
¹⁰ Stern discipline awaits anyone who leaves the path;
   the one who hates correction will die.
¹¹ Death and Destruction lie open before the Lord—
   how much more do human hearts!
¹² Mockers resent correction,
   so they avoid the wise.
¹³ A happy heart makes the face cheerful,
   but heartache crushes the spirit.
¹⁴ The discerning heart seeks knowledge,
   but the mouth of a fool feeds on folly.
¹⁵ All the days of the oppressed are wretched,
   but the cheerful heart has a continual feast.
¹⁶ Better a little with the fear of the Lord
   than great wealth with turmoil.
¹⁷ Better a small serving of vegetables with love
   than a fattened calf with hatred.

¹⁸ A hot-tempered person stirs up conflict,
   but the one who is patient calms a quarrel.
¹⁹ The way of the sluggard is blocked with thorns,
   but the path of the upright is a highway.
²⁰ A wise son brings joy to his father,
   but a foolish man despises his mother.
²¹ Folly brings joy to one who has no sense,
   but whoever has understanding keeps a straight course.
²² Plans fail for lack of counsel,
   but with many advisers they succeed.
²³ A person finds joy in giving an apt reply—
   and how good is a timely word!
²⁴ The path of life leads upward for the prudent
   to keep them from going down to the realm of the dead.
²⁵ The Lord tears down the house of the proud,
   but he sets the widow's boundary stones in place.
²⁶ The Lord detests the thoughts of the wicked,
   but gracious words are pure in his sight.
²⁷ The greedy bring ruin to their households,
   but the one who hates bribes will live.
²⁸ The heart of the righteous weighs its answers,
   but the mouth of the wicked gushes evil.
²⁹ The Lord is far from the wicked,
   but he hears the prayer of the righteous.
³⁰ Light in a messenger's eyes brings joy to the heart,
   and good news gives health to the bones.
³¹ Whoever heeds life-giving correction
   will be at home among the wise.
³² Those who disregard discipline despise themselves,
   but the one who heeds correction gains understanding.
³³ Wisdom's instruction is to fear the Lord,
   and humility comes before honor.

MEDITATE & REFLECT

_____

_____

_____

_____

_____

_____

_____

_____

_____

_____

_____

_____

_____

_____

_____

Before you go forward, you have to go back. You are not going back to mourn; you are going back to break. To break open what has been closed and concealed and, in some sense, protected from further evaluation. When you evaluate anything, you are going in to see what it's all about, to address what is and what's to come of it, to see whether it should stay where it is or if it should change.

When you go back and address one thing, you are giving God permission to get it all. What is God getting? He is getting all of the infections out so that the infection will stop affecting your life. The repercussions of being affected are infecting the purposeful plans that God has for your life. Who you are in fullness cannot fully emerge because of everything around it that is causing it not to come forth and shine and be what it is supposed to be.

Are you tired of starting things and not completing them? Are you tired of running and then breaking your ankle or foot, and having to take a break to heal? Have you built up the fortitude and stamina to run and thrive? If you had seen the pothole that you fell into, you would have avoided the fall, therefore avoiding the break. And in this sense, the break means time. Time is of the essence and is very important.

Because you have not been broken in the sense of opening to what has not been addressed, the broken part of you is infected and intentionally hidden. You can't address what you can't see. A lot of times we associate what we feel with what we see. God knows all things, and we find ourselves often running away from God, the seer of all things. He sees your current state and created the outcome before we even started the path. If we are in denial about a situation, we won't see it for what it really is. This is why all senses must be sanctified because all senses have been affected by trauma.

God does deal with us through our emotions. Emotions are a good indicator of God speaking to us and revealing information to us, but if those senses are infected by the trauma that was not addressed, how can you properly hear or see correctly? When the area that has not been broken by God is unaddressed, it can hinder our ability to see, hear, taste, or feel effectively. Some things that we think are good, that sometimes feel good in the moment, are not always good for you.

* * *

Have you ever allowed your pain to choose for you? Have you allowed how you feel in the moment to make crucial decisions that can ultimately derail your destiny?

_____

_____

_____

_____

_____

_____

_____

_____

_____

We cannot continue to allow pain to speak louder than purpose. Pain can sometimes help us tap into our purpose because it presses us more into the presence of God. Pain pushes us closer to our divine help, which is our Lord, Jesus Christ. So, we are going to take a journey back to identify where the trauma started, where the pain began, and what God said the expected end should be. We are not going back to just look back and ponder, but to allow God to take you back to heal. It's time to break open what has been concealed for a long time.

Consider the phrase, "Don't forget about me." Initially, we might interpret it as a self-centered plea. However, reflecting on the biblical story of Jesus staying back in Jerusalem while His parents were unaware, we witness a different perspective. Jesus, divine and human, the Savior of the world, returned to Jerusalem to mature naturally and spiritually until the appointed time. Is it your appointed time to heal? If you are reading this book, then the answer is *yes*!

"When they had finished the days, as they returned, the Boy Jesus lingered behind in Jerusalem. And Joseph and His mother did not know it; but supposing Him to have been in the company, they went a day's journey, and sought Him among their relatives and acquaintances. So when they did not find Him, they returned to Jerusalem, seeking Him. Now so it was that after three days they found Him in the temple, sitting in the midst of the teachers, both listening to them and asking them questions. And all who heard Him were astonished at His understanding and answers. And when they saw Him, they were amazed; and His mother said to Him, 'Son, why have You done this to us? Look, Your father and I have sought You anxiously.' And He said to them, 'Why did you seek Me? Did you not know that I must be about My Father's business?' But they did not understand the statement which He spoke to them. Then He went down with them and came to Nazareth, and was subject to them, but His mother kept all these things in her heart."

— *LUKE 2:43-51*

Jesus humbled himself and waited for the appointed time to be revealed. How many of us are going to go through that process? I went through that process, and while I'm writing this, I'm going through that process. The Lord gave me the directive to take a sabbatical from many things that I was doing in ministry because of the surgery that He was performing in my heart. Some things happened in my life, internally, which required me to pause, reflect, and allow God to heal me so that I could become whole. When it was time for me to reintroduce myself to the world, it would be as new, improved Crystal. Some people are not willing to give it all up. Give it back to God, and He will make it better than it was before. I'm talking about a major spiritual upgrade. Some things worked before that will not work in this season. If we don't allow God to stop us from operating in this manner, we will not experience the greater. Sometimes what we're doing is not wrong. It's just not right for now. What is God saying now? What is your purpose now? What is going to work to help facilitate the new you, the powerful force, and bring others into their new? Let's investigate this a little further.

Navigating Life's Roadway

Traveling down life's highway, we find ourselves in a constant balancing act. It's as if our focus is divided between what lies ahead and what lingers behind us. Like a rearview mirror, the past is out of our forefront but never entirely out of sight. When you don't have forward focus in view, it can be rather difficult to move forward in life with a clear mindset.

Picture this: as I glance at the rearview, my eyes remain fixed on what lies ahead, yet I am aware of the need to stay mindful of what has happened behind me. It is in this delicate place between reflection and anticipation that we find ourselves looking to avoid potential incidents, trying to stay cautious and safe on this journey. But just like on the road, giving too much attention to what's behind can be detrimental. If we stare too long into the rearview, we risk crashing into the obstacles ahead. It is here, in this space, that paranoia and anxiety can set in. These blind spots of the mind can cloud our judgment and hinder our progress, causing us to question every turn we take. However, we must overcome fear and continue living forward. Though there may be uncertainties and challenges we encounter, we must remember to cast our cares upon the Lord.

Philippians 4:7 tells us, "And the peace of God, which transcends all understanding, will guard your hearts and your minds in Christ Jesus." Remember that we look into the rearview not as an act of dwelling on the past, but as a means of learning from our past experiences. It is in this process that we gain a better understanding of our journey, avoiding past mistakes and seeking the wisdom of God to make better choices. As we journey forth, sometimes we find ourselves gripped in fear instead of walking in confidence, being reminded that every step we take according to God's plan will work out in our favor. When we have a mindset outside of God's will, it opens us up to a plan B. The road ahead may be unpredictable, but if we trust in the Lord and cast our anxieties upon Him, He will sustain us.

Psalm 55:22 reassures us that the Lord will strengthen us, ensuring that the righteous will never be shaken. Are you ready to embark on this unprecedented journey with our eyes fixed on the Lord, our hearts steadfast in faith, and a readiness to overcome any roadblocks that hinder our progress?

I remember in times past asking the Lord to erase my memory. I didn't want to feel the pain of the trauma from the past. My memory was my enemy. In those times of trauma, I didn't fully practice casting my cares; I preached it and released godly counsel to others, but I found myself in tight places where I refused to take advantage of the application. We have to intentionally allow God to renew our minds, understanding that this will require repeated programming. We can tap into the reservoir of our subconscious and allow God to deal with what has been stored up. It's time to experience God's transformative power.

The mind, also known as the mental faculty, is responsible for various cognitive functions such as thinking, imagining, remembering, willing, and sensing. It encompasses a set of abilities that enable these processes to occur. The mind is closely associated with the experience of perception, pleasure, pain, belief, desire, intention, and emotion, involving both conscious and non-conscious states, with both sensory and non-sensory experiences. Attempting to transition from one lifestyle to another can be overwhelmingly challenging for the mind.

In the process, you find yourself flowing in a path that aligns with your way of living. It's difficult not to conform to the system that dominates the world. Because of this, your mind experiences a glitch, causing a malfunction in its operating system. Using computers as a reference point: eventually, the system crashes, leaving you with the task of rebuilding from scratch. Obtaining a new hard drive serves as the equivalent of acquiring a completely new computer. Throughout this process, everything that was previously stored is erased. Nevertheless, similar to how Apple stores data in the cloud, the subconscious mind retains information, ready to be accessed and utilized in rebuilding or reminding.

In a natural sense, it is easier to dismiss things that could potentially ruin what you are trying to develop in foresight by experience, logical views, or predominantly a prophetic word from the Lord. Rebuilding or reprogramming cannot be done without being born again into a new life. Even after being born again, we have different stages in our lives where this process is ongoing. In the process of being discipled, we have to allow God to sanctify us, which will require separation from people, places, things, and even our own mindset. Godly wisdom and maturity will help aid in the process of healing. Bringing traumatic or difficult ordeals to the forefront of your mind can foster an environment of healing or cause further damage if not assisted with strong godly counsel or being equipped within with the help of the Holy Spirit to lead and guide in the right path towards healing.

"Therefore, if anyone is in Christ, he is a new creation; old things have passed away; behold, all things have become new."

— 2 CORINTHIANS 5:17

Due to the complexities of our humanistic minds, distractions, or lack of communion with God, it can sometimes be challenging to comprehend the messages God is conveying to us. That is why settling ourselves down is an essential starting point that God wants me to emphasize. Paul discusses the inner battle that takes place within us.

"But there is another power within me that is at war with my mind. This power makes me a slave to the sin that is still within me."

— ROMANS 7:23

Transformation happens through instruction and us actively engaging in the presence of God. Spending time with God, surrounding yourself with a community—whether it be church or support groups, whatever atmosphere can foster healing and growth in all areas. We must consider the entirety of our existence as human beings, composed of the body, mind, heart, soul, and spirit. All of these aspects contribute to our identity and determine how we live our lives. Each area is significant as we seek to fulfill God's plan for our lives. The Holy Spirit serves as the driving force through which this divine alignment can occur. What a blessing to have such a transformational gift in the person of the Holy Spirit as our guide. If we allow any other aspect of ourselves to control our actions, without the guidance of the Holy Spirit, complications arise. The reason why these other areas can lead us astray is often rooted in past traumas that have influenced our emotional state, causing it to take complete control in times of vulnerability.

THE POWER OF THE MIND AND OBEDIENCE TO ABBA FATHER

I didn't know I had it in me! I once preached a message that carried a powerful revelation that changed my life. When different things begin to come up in your life and are triggered by traumatic offenses, your heart begins to be exposed, and you begin to react to what was there all along. It was suppressed, hidden, locked away, not wanting to be felt, acknowledged, or recognized. If we are honest, we wanted it to go away and thought it was gone. Though memory loss for essential information is rare, we often forget minor details. Our memory seldom forgets essential things like going to work or taking care of our families. But sometimes, we forget to get the ketchup or the bread during a visit to the market, or we lock the keys in the car. These minor forgetfulness highlight the battle between the major and minor things we choose to remember.

Our short-term memory often frustrates us when we have many things to do and remember. But then we have that memory of trauma that happened 17 years ago, which can change our mindset and mood immediately and sometimes control our current actions in the moment of the thought. We say to ourselves that if we can forget it or put it in the back of our mind—which we really mean our subconscious mind—then it won't hurt anymore. But this method of coping is unhealthy and can cause further damage, opening the door for so many other clusters of spirits that can press on us later in life. It's not ironic that these things will start to fester when you're at the prime of your life, and then you will confess, "I didn't know I had it in me, still."

Years ago, I received a divine revelation to pray for my subconscious mind. At the time, I didn't fully comprehend the significance until I delved into studying the complexities of the mind and brain. This journey began when my son was diagnosed with developmental delay, and I started interceding for every area of his brain. It was soon after intercession that much breakthrough happened for him. He is now 15 years old, author of four books, an honor roll student excelling in every area of his life, and it was nothing but the grace and mercy of God.

The subconscious mind plays a significant role in our lives. It comprises approximately 95% of our brain power and controls our bodily functions, memories, and behaviors. Understanding its processes can be helpful in our lives. How do we reprogram our minds? Repetition is key to programming the subconscious mind. By listening to and repeating what we want to reprogram, we can shape our thought patterns and align ourselves with God's Word.

Romans 10:17 tells us that faith comes from hearing, and hearing comes from the Word of God. It is often said that the most opportune times to program our subconscious minds are in the morning upon waking up and before going to sleep. These are the moments when our minds are more receptive to new information and capable of assimilating it into our belief systems.

"In the morning, Lord, you hear my voice; in the morning I lay my requests before you and wait expectantly."

— PSALM 5:3

"Early will I seek thee; so shall my spirit wait on thee early."

— PSALM 63:1

"I rise before dawn and cry out for help; I put my hope in your word."

— PSALM 119:147-148

"Be angry, and do not sin. Meditate within your heart on your bed and be still. Offer sacrifices of righteousness and trust in the Lord."

— PSALM 4:4

"I lie down in the darkness, yet I remember you. The night is filled with your whispers, and I pray to you, like one pouring out a prayer to you."

— PSALM 63:6-7

Our physical bodies have a natural rhythm, which regulates our sleep-wake cycles and bodily functions, with the brain being most active in the morning and evening. This natural cycle aligns with the biblical concept of praying in the morning (Psalm 5:3) and at night (Psalm 63:6-7), suggesting that God designed our bodies to be receptive to prayer during these times.

By programming our subconscious minds during these periods, we can take advantage of what God enlightens us about concerning our physical bodies to deepen our connection with God and rewire our minds for spiritual growth. It's important to note that this doesn't mean that we should only pray during these times, but rather that God is always available to hear our prayers throughout the day, and incorporating morning and evening prayer into our daily routine can be a powerful way to stay connected with Him.

Our subconscious mind acts as a memory bank, storing every experience we've ever had. Its capacity is limitless, making it a powerful force within us having the mind of Christ. However, to tap into its full potential, we must discipline ourselves. It takes natural discipline to experience supernatural occurrences. When we align our minds with God's Word, we can translate His promises into our lives. We must allow the mind of Christ to guide our thoughts and actions.

Our souls have the capacity to remember and store experiences and knowledge.

> *"I praise you because I am fearfully and wonderfully made; your works are wonderful, I know that full well. My frame was not hidden from you when I was made in the secret place. When I was woven together in the depths of the earth, your eyes saw my unformed body. All the days ordained for me were written in your book and planned before a single one of them began."*
>
> — PSALM 139:14-16

God has a complete record of our lives, including our memories and experiences.

> *"See, I have inscribed you on the palms of my hands; your walls are continually before me."*
>
> — ISAIAH 49:16

God has a deep connection with us and has a record of our experiences and memories. The things that God highlights and wants us to remember at particular times in our lives are either to teach us a lesson, to draw our attention to it, or to bring it to the surface so that we can receive healing or closure. Whatever it may be, there is nothing that has happened in our lives that God does not know about, and if, in time, He chooses to allow those memories to come to the surface, there is a purpose.

We also have to understand that the enemy of our souls will try to remind us of things that have happened in our lives and keep us entertained by trying to keep our minds in the same continuous, repeated mindset, preventing us from thinking differently. Thinking differently will never be based upon what we have experienced, but it can be based on what we've learned from the experience, allowing us to grow because of it.

There are aspects of life we may want to forget because they have caused us great pain. However, even if we were to erase those memories, they would still affect our emotions, decision-making, heart, physical body, and spirit. Our experiences shape us and determine the outcomes and flow of our lives.

While we are one body, we have different parts that need special attention. Just as we have a primary doctor and sometimes need to seek a specialist, so too must we seek the intimacy and obedience of our Heavenly Father, Abba. Abba is more than just having an intimate relationship with our Father; it also implies obedience. Abba is like the English term "Sir" rather than "Daddy." It speaks of authority and submission.

Addressing the cry within us and releasing it according to our understanding of Abba requires both intimacy and obedience. He is our provider, but also the one who gives instructions. Just as a plane needs a straight path to gain speed and altitude, we can't ignore our problems or waver in our obedience. We must respond to what Abba does and who He is by obeying His instructions. In the chapters to come, we will explore the power of obedience and aligning our minds with God's Word.

THE CRY OF UNRESOLVED TRAUMA AND DEAD DREAMS

The deep cry, "Don't forget about me," could stem from two sources: unresolved traumas or dead dreams and visions. Unresolved traumas often reside in our subconscious minds, affecting our emotions, physical bodies, relationships, and decision-making. If left unaddressed, they can silence a part of ourselves that needs attention, development, and healing—like a child crying out within us, lost and voiceless. When traumas kill our dreams and visions, we feel unseen and unheard. Until we confront these unresolved issues, we cannot grow in the things of God or move forward in life.

When we first have a dream or vision, it's on the ground level, waiting to take off and soar. But often, we let go of these dreams and forget about them. Unaddressed traumas and dead dreams can hinder us from focusing on our Kingdom assignments. Why do we let these dreams go?

- Lack of confidence?
- Lack of support?

God's power is not meant to feed our egos; it's meant to demonstrate His glory. Our dreams, visions, and talents are not for selfish ambition but are intended to help others start or begin again. It's time to silence the noise of discouragement and embrace the sound of freedom, humbling ourselves before the Lord and relying solely on His power to carry out everything He's given us to do.

Unresolved issues can have a voice because they stem from unhealed wounds that have not been properly addressed. When we fail to investigate the source of our pain and allow God to work in those areas, unresolved issues can continue to manifest in our lives. These unresolved issues often reveal themselves in our uncontrolled responses and behaviors, showing that the wounds are still present and affecting us. To truly grow in the things of God, we must allow Him to heal these deep-rooted issues, enabling us to focus on our Kingdom assignments and respond in a healed, godly manner.

It is crucial not to ignore these issues, as they can continue to impact us negatively and prevent us from moving forward in our lives. When these issues are resolved, we can confidently step into our identity in Christ and move forward in our purpose.

In Ezekiel 16, God speaks about the bitterness and brokenness within us. Even after we are born again, we need to undergo a process of sanctification. We are affected by our past and bloodline patterns, but through sanctification, God can work these things out of us. He calls us to trust Him, let go of our fleshly desires, build on His foundation, and follow Him.

Ezekiel 16

[1] The word of the Lord came to me:

[2] "Son of man, confront Jerusalem with her detestable practices

[3] and say, 'This is what the Sovereign Lord says to Jerusalem: Your ancestry and birth were in the land of the Canaanites; your father was an Amorite and your mother a Hittite.

[4] On the day you were born your cord was not cut, nor were you washed with water to make you clean, nor were you rubbed with salt or wrapped in cloths.

[5] No one looked on you with pity or had compassion enough to do any of these things for you. Rather, you were thrown out into the open field, for on the day you were born you were despised.

[6] "'Then I passed by and saw you kicking about in your blood, and as you lay there in your blood I said to you, "Live!"

[7] I made you grow like a plant of the field. You grew and developed and entered puberty. Your breasts had formed and your hair had grown, yet you were stark naked.

[8] "'Later I passed by, and when I looked at you and saw that you were old enough for love, I spread the corner of my garment over you and covered your naked body. I gave you my solemn oath and entered into a covenant with you, declares the Sovereign Lord, and you became mine.

[9] "'I bathed you with water and washed the blood from you and put ointments on you.

[10] I clothed you with an embroidered dress and put sandals of fine leather on you. I dressed you in fine linen and covered you with costly garments.

[11] I adorned you with jewelry: I put bracelets on your arms and a necklace around your neck,

[12] and I put a ring on your nose, earrings on your ears and a beautiful crown on your head.

[13] So you were adorned with gold and silver; your clothes were of fine linen and costly fabric and embroidered cloth. Your food

was honey, olive oil and the finest flour. You became very beautiful and rose to be a queen.

¹⁴ And your fame spread among the nations on account of your beauty, because the splendor I had given you made your beauty perfect, declares the Sovereign Lord.

¹⁵ "'But you trusted in your beauty and used your fame to become a prostitute. You lavished your favors on anyone who passed by and your beauty became his.

¹⁶ You took some of your garments to make gaudy high places, where you carried on your prostitution. You went to him, and he possessed your beauty.

¹⁷ You also took the fine jewelry I gave you, the jewelry made of my gold and silver, and you made for yourself male idols and engaged in prostitution with them.

¹⁸ And you took your embroidered clothes to put on them, and you offered my oil and incense before them.

¹⁹ Also the food I provided for you—the flour, olive oil and honey I gave you to eat—you offered as fragrant incense before them. That is what happened, declares the Sovereign Lord.

SPIRITUAL ANCESTORS

Ezekiel 16 begins with a description of humanity; this is a reminder of our natural state, separate from God and prone to rebellion. This was also confirmed in Jeremiah 2:14.

"Your first father was Hittite, and your prophet was Amorite."

— JEREMIAH 2:14

Describing the Israelites' spiritual ancestors, the text in Ezekiel 16:1-2 identifies their earliest roots as coming from the Hittites and Amorites, both of which were ancient Near Eastern cultures. The names of these two ancient Mesopotamian city-states, Amorite and Hittite, are interpreted as having meanings that describe the character or nature of their people—Amorite being associated with rebellion, bitterness, and babbling, and Hittite being associated with brokenness or fear. These names also refer to specific ancient cultures and civilizations that once thrived in the Middle East, offering a glimpse into the complex societies that existed in this region.

It's important to acknowledge and be mindful of the generational and cultural backgrounds in our lives, whether through blood or association. However, there are certain things we must no longer embrace in order to move forward, and I believe that God is opening our eyes to see what needs to be left behind and what needs to be cultivated and made fruitful.

THE UNADDRESSED WOUND

The text in Ezekiel 16:4-5 flows into the theme of birth, but not just any birth. The cord that was supposed to be cut at birth was not, symbolizing the things we have adopted as our own rather than surrendering to God's sanctifying process. We are not washed with water, rubbed with salt, or wrapped in cloths, but instead left in the open field, exposed and despised. It was masked yet exposed, for God sees all things. You were birthed out in the open, and your brokenness was visible. The cord of bitterness was not cut because you rebelled against the cutting away. God desires for us to be washed daily in His word so that we can be purified from all lust and clothed in righteousness. Don't run away from the process—the cutting and pruning—it will benefit you in the days, weeks, months, and years to come.

THE BLOOD OF LIFE

The text in Ezekiel 16:6-7 reveals the image of blood that is used throughout the passage to symbolize life. Blood symbolizes life. Once blood leaves your body, it becomes contaminated. The life you once knew has left you and is no longer benefiting you. The blood has left us, and we are left in a dead situation. Another word for kicking is wallowing; we must determine that we will no longer wallow in situations that are fruitless. What unaddressed wound caused us to bleed out?

This is a powerful reminder of the ways in which we have been wounded and how we continue to wallow in those wounds rather than seeking healing and restoration.

GOD'S WORD OF LIFE

The text in Ezekiel 16:8-14 refers to God's Word of life! But then comes God's word of life: "Live!" This is a call to surrender to God's sovereignty and to trust in His plan for our lives. It's not just a call to life—it's also a call to restoration. We are told that we are being restored, that we are being brought back from the dead. The situation may be dead, but the unaddressed wound is on life support, meaning it's time to stop sustaining the dead places. After you decide to live, God will begin to reveal to you what shall be. You have bled out past discrepancies; now you're being restored into a new place.

GROWTH AND DEVELOPMENT

God continues to care for us as we grow and develop. We are nourished, clothed, adorned, and beautified. But despite this care, we often turn away from God and trust in our own beauty and fame. God is calling us out of our idolatry and our tendency to rely on our appearances rather than on His sovereignty. At times, due to insecurity and not recognizing our value in the spirit, we have allowed ourselves to be taken advantage of and have sold ourselves out to the world instead of remaining faithful to God.

THE CALL TO SURRENDER

Before we take off our old selves and put on our new selves, we must surrender to God's sovereignty and trust in His plan for our lives. We must stop wallowing in our wounds and seek healing and restoration. Sometimes, we trust in the illusion of freedom based on appearances, but were we truly free? Are we free now? We must trust in God's word of life rather than relying on our own perceptions.

God is our hope and redemption. He sees us in all our brokenness and calls us to surrender and repentance. He offers us a word of life and restoration, promising to heal our wounds and make us whole again. In this significant season of walking with the Lord, remember that before you can take off, you have to take off what no longer fosters growth and progression in your life. God will break us down to build us up, and part of this process involves burying our past and leaving it behind. When we bury our past, we can move forward into God's promises for us.

Although the burial process may be painful, we will soar to new heights when we emerge on the other side. God wants us to trust Him, act in faith, and obey His Word. He has given us the formula for healing, deliverance, and freedom. All we need to do is believe and receive by faith. We cannot correct or fix something that He has already finished for us. Once we bury our past, we can receive the promises that God has for us. As we grow closer to God, He will resolve our traumas and awaken our dreams, allowing us to experience a spiritual tsunami that transforms our lives.

> *"The God who stirs up the sea and causes waves to roar is near to those who call on Him."*
>
> — PSALM 107:25

God wants us to grow in our character and integrity and soar to new heights. In 1 Corinthians 3:11-15, we read about building on the foundation of Jesus Christ. Each one's work will be made manifest, and it will be revealed by fire, and the fire will test what sort of work each one has done. If the work that anyone has built on the foundation survives, he will receive a reward. If anyone's work is burned up, he will suffer loss, though he himself will be saved, but only as through fire.

> *"For no one can lay any foundation other than the one already laid, which is Jesus Christ. If anyone builds on this foundation using gold, silver, costly stones, wood, hay or straw, their work will be shown for what it is, because the Day will bring it to light. It will be revealed with fire, and the fire will test the quality of each person's work. If what has been built survives, the builder will receive a reward. If it is burned up, the*

builder will suffer loss but yet will be saved—even though only as one escaping through the flames."

— 1 CORINTHIANS 3:11-15

SOAR INTO WHOLENESS

It's time to look back, not as Lot's wife did, but at the parts of ourselves that we've left behind, bruised and damaged. I want to explore the issue with Lot's wife and how it may have had a lasting impact on what happened with Lot and their children.

Genesis 19:12-26

12 The two men said to Lot, "Do you have anyone else here— sons-in-law, sons or daughters, or anyone else in the city who belongs to you? Get them out of here,

13 because we are going to destroy this place. The outcry to the Lord against its people is so great that he has sent us to destroy it."

14 So Lot went out and spoke to his sons-in-law, who were pledged to marry his daughters. He said, "Hurry and get out of this place, because the Lord is about to destroy the city!" But his sons-in-law thought he was joking.

15 With the coming of dawn, the angels urged Lot, saying, "Hurry! Take your wife and your two daughters who are here, or you will be swept away when the city is punished."

16 When he hesitated, the men grasped his hand and the hands of his wife and of his two daughters and led them safely out of the city, for the Lord was merciful to them.

17 As soon as they had brought them out, one of them said, "Flee for your lives! Don't look back, and don't stop anywhere in the plain! Flee to the mountains or you will be swept away!"

18 But Lot said to them, "No, my lords, please! 19 Your servant has found favor in your eyes, and you have shown great kind-

ness to me in sparing my life. But I can't flee to the mountains; this disaster will overtake me, and I'll die.

²⁰ Look, here is a town near enough to run to, and it is small. Let me flee to it—it is very small, isn't it? Then my life will be spared."

²¹ He said to him, "Very well, I will grant this request too; I will not overthrow the town you speak of.

²² But flee there quickly, because I cannot do anything until you reach it." (That is why the town was called Zoar.)

²³ By the time Lot reached Zoar, the sun had risen over the land.

²⁴ Then the Lord rained down burning sulfur on Sodom and Gomorrah—from the Lord out of the heavens.

²⁵ Thus he overthrew those cities and the entire plain, destroying all those living in the cities—and also the vegetation in the land.

²⁶ But Lot's wife looked back, and she became a pillar of salt.

Let's take a moment to explore how Lot arrived at the place he did. I will provide some context to build the foundation of this explanation. Abraham was instructed to leave his country and his family and go to a place he did not know, where God promised to make him the father of many nations.

Abraham's Charge to Leave His Country:

"Now the Lord said to Abram, 'Go from your country, your people and your father's household to the land I will show you. I will make you a great nation and I will bless you; I will make your name great, and you will be a blessing. I will bless those who bless you, and whoever curses you I will curse; and all peoples on earth will be blessed through you, because you have obeyed me.'"

— Genesis 12:1-3

Lot was Abraham's Wife's Brother's Son:

> *"While his father Terah was still alive, Haran died in Ur of the Chaldeans, in the land of his birth. Abram and Nahor both married. The name of Abram's wife was Sarai, and the name of Nahor's wife was Milkah; she was the daughter of Haran, the father of both Milkah and Iskah. Now Sarai was childless because she was not able to conceive. Terah took his son Abram, his grandson Lot son of Haran, and his daughter-in-law Sarai, the wife of his son Abram, and together they set out from Ur of the Chaldeans to go to Canaan. But when they came to Harran, they settled there. Terah lived 205 years, and he died in Harran."*

> — GENESIS 11:28-32

Regarding Lot's relationship with Abraham, it is indeed stated that Haran died, which could suggest that Lot was living with Abraham. Many have discussed how Abraham taking Lot with him might not have been part of God's plan, especially given the events that transpired. However, it's possible that Abraham took Lot with him because he was part of his family and perhaps even a protégé. It's clear that Abraham had a deep affection for him.

Lot may have been living with Abraham and Sarah because of Haran's death, which would have left him without a family to return to. Since Abraham and Nahor took their father Terah's place, it's likely that Abraham felt a sense of responsibility to care for his nephew, Lot.

An interesting point to note is that Haran is mentioned as the father of Lot in Genesis 11:27, and the place where Terah's family lived was named Haran in Genesis 11:31. Some scholars suggest that the name "Haran" might be derived from the Hebrew word "harar," meaning "parched" or "dry," or possibly from the Akkadian word "charana," meaning "a road." This provides fascinating insight into the possible origins of Haran's name. Haran was a road they traveled, but it was not the final destination. It was not a land of fruitfulness; rather, it was the place where someone died. In our context, we might interpret this as a place where something dies, and God then sends us on our journey to His promise without access to that which has passed.

Not only did Abraham's nephew go with him, but his father Terah did as well, highlighting the significance of family ties in this context. Both Lot's father and grandfather died, leaving Abraham as the only male figure in Lot's life. Lot's connection to Abraham's blessing and prosperity is evident in how his own family and possessions grew abundantly. He prospered as he admired Abraham's wisdom and how he successfully became a wealthy man. Their prosperity was so great that they had to separate due to conflicts over their flocks.

Genesis 13:5-13

⁵ Now Lot, who was moving about with Abram, also had flocks and herds and tents.

⁶ But the land could not support them while they stayed together, for their possessions were so great that they were not able to stay together.

⁷ And quarreling arose between Abram's herders and Lot's. The Canaanites and Perizzites were also living in the land at that time.

⁸ So Abram said to Lot, "Let's not have any quarreling between you and me, or between your herders and mine, for we are close relatives.

⁹ Is not the whole land before you? Let's part company. If you go to the left, I'll go to the right; if you go to the right, I'll go to the left."

¹⁰ Lot looked around and saw that the whole plain of the Jordan toward Zoar was well watered, like the garden of the Lord, like the land of Egypt. (This was before the Lorddestroyed Sodom and Gomorrah.)

¹¹ So Lot chose for himself the whole plain of the Jordan and set out toward the east. The two men parted company:

¹² Abram lived in the land of Canaan,while Lot lived among the cities of the plain and pitched his tents near Sodom.

¹³ Now the people of Sodom were wicked and were sinning greatly against the Lord.

Let's hone in on Lot's reasoning behind the land he chose to travel to.

"Lot looked around and saw that the whole plain of the Jordan toward Zoar was well watered, like the garden of the Lord, like the land of Egypt. (This was before the Lord destroyed Sodom and Gomorrah.) So Lot chose for himself the whole plain of the Jordan and set out toward the east."

— GENESIS 13:10-11

First, I want to point out that Lot did not pray before choosing where to go next. He observed that the land looked like the garden of the Lord and like the land of Egypt. If we consider the distinction between the two, he may have been comparing the garden of the Lord to the Garden of Eden, being in the presence of God. However, he also compared it to Egypt, which was once a place of bondage for the Israelites. How ironic is that? He made this distinct comparison at the time of his decision. We should take a closer look at what we can learn from this text, especially as it relates to our wholeness and our tendency to look back on what was. Egypt represents the past, while Canaan, the promise, represents the future. We cannot make decisions based on appearances alone; instead, we must make decisions based on what God says, seeking His guidance in every season of our lives.

Lot's decision to settle near Sodom and Gomorrah may not have been a wise one, and it ultimately led to devastating consequences for his family. This serves as a powerful reminder that even when we are blessed with God's favor, our choices and decisions can still have negative outcomes. Consider the reasoning behind Lot's daughters intentionally getting their father drunk because they wanted to have children, and their potential husbands were not willing to leave when Lot warned them. This could have meant that the lineage might have ended at this point. If Lot's wife had still been in the picture, this might not have happened because she would have been present to prevent her daughters from doing what they did to their father. The deep-rooted issue here is incest, which trickled down through the generations.

Could it be that Lot's wife was in a state of unbelief when she looked back? The world she knew, the life she had, and the family she built in that place were being destroyed, and she was running toward an uncertain future. This teaches us a valuable lesson: there are times in our lives when the place we are in is not conducive to what God is releasing upon us, and staying in a place of complacency could endanger our purpose from being fulfilled. Looking back can sometimes cripple us because we are so accustomed to where we are. We can learn many lessons from this passage and should seek the Lord and pray for divine revelation as we read, study, and meditate on His word daily. God's favor and redemption are evident throughout this story. Despite the destruction of Sodom and Gomorrah, Lot's family members—except for his wife—were spared, and Abraham's faithfulness was rewarded. It's a testament to God's sovereignty and mercy, even amid human failure and imperfection.

Lot's Daughters Plotted to Sleep with Their Father:

> *"Now the two daughters of Lot became pregnant by their father. The older one gave birth to a son and named him Moab, saying, 'He is the father of my people.' The younger one gave birth to a son and named him Ben-Ammi, saying, 'He is the father of my son.'"*

> — GENESIS 19:37-38

Lot's daughters, Zoar and Adoquim, bore him two children, Moab and Ben-Ammi. These children became the ancestors of the Moabites and Ammonites, two nations known for their conflicts with the Israelites in the Old Testament.

The conflict between the Moabites, Ammonites, and Israel is mentioned in several places in the Bible.

1. *Numbers 21:21-25*: This passage describes the Israelites'

conquest of the kingdom of Sihon, which was ruled by the Amorite king Og. After conquering Sihon, the Israelites then defeated the Moabites, who were led by King Balak.

2. *Deuteronomy 2:9-37:* This passage describes the Israelites' journey through the land of Moab and their conflicts with the Moabites. It also mentions the Israelites' conquest of the city of Heshbon, which was originally ruled by the Amorites.

3. *Deuteronomy 3:1-7:* This passage describes the Israelites' conquest of the kingdom of Og, which was located in the region of Bashan. The Moabites and Ammonites are mentioned as being present in the region at the time.

4. *Judges 3:12-30*: This passage describes the Israelites' conflict with the king of Moab, Eglon, who oppressed them for 18 years. The Ammonites are also mentioned as being present in the region at the time.

5. *1 Kings 11:1-5*: This passage describes how King Solomon, who was a descendant of David, married a Moabite woman named Naamah, who was from Bethlehem. The Moabites are also mentioned as being present in the region during this time.

The decisions we make now may not immediately affect us, but they can have a long-term negative impact on the generations that come after us. So, let's be prayerful and mindful of our current positioning, and pray that our steps are continuously ordered by the Lord. We need to allow God to show us the parts of our lives that no longer serve us and ignite the areas that are ready to launch into something greater. It's time to gather what you need so you can move forward to where God is leading you now!

While the death of Terah occurred before Abraham walked into what God had promised him, this story might resonate with those who have experienced loss—not just the loss of a loved one, but perhaps the death of a career, a marriage, or the old version of yourself. Whatever the

loss may be, don't let it stop you from moving on to the new, resurrected journey that is unfolding before your eyes. There is more within
you than you realize.

As I stated in the previous chapter, "I didn't know I had it in me" is
a sentiment that can go unspoken but is deeply felt. I didn't realize that
the baggage and the purpose were different parts of me. We are made up
of compartments—our physical bodies, spirits, souls, hearts, and minds.
Each part needs to be cultivated and nurtured by the Word.

DEATH BEFORE THE PROMISE

One thing that stood out to me was that Terah, though set on reaching
the promised land with Abraham, died before he arrived. I know this
must have been a difficult time for Abraham, losing both his brother
and his father. Yet, he still had a mission and was determined to
complete it. You are on your way to a new place, bound to break
records, accomplish goals, and push past all the hindrances that stopped
you before—even if the obstacle is the person in the mirror. God is
building you so that your capacity to receive will be greater.

God said, "I'm giving you foreknowledge of what's coming ahead."
Foreknowledge refers to the knowledge that God has of future events,
people, and circumstances. It is God's knowledge of what will happen
before it actually occurs. God is omniscient, meaning He knows everything—past, present, and future.

"According to the foreknowledge of God the Father..."

— 1 PETER 1:2

"For those whom he foreknew he also predestined..."

— ROMANS 8:29

"Now that you have come to know God, or rather to be known by God..."

— GALATIANS 4:9

In these scriptures, foreknowledge is described as God's knowledge of people, their salvation, calling, and destiny. God is sovereign and has a plan for His creation. His plans are not random or haphazard but are based on His perfect knowledge and wisdom. It is comforting to know that God has a plan for us, and that He is always in control, knowing what is best for us. So today, be encouraged and don't lose hope, because God has a plan for our lives and is working out our salvation in accordance with His will.

Did you know that every part of you needs to be in alignment and agreement with God and His purpose? Mark 12:30 emphasizes loving God with all your heart, soul, mind, and strength. Philippians 4:7 speaks of the peace of God guarding our hearts and minds. Romans 12:2 highlights the importance of renewing our minds to discern God's will. And 1 Corinthians 6:19-20 reminds us that our bodies are temples of the Holy Spirit and should be honored.

I had to personally walk through a process where I was strong and gifted in one area while the rest needed fine-tuning. We can't soar to the highest altitude if one wing is damaged. Breakthrough is intentional, often happening simultaneously in different areas of our lives. When you see a persistent problem, discipline is key. Seek the Lord and trust Him to remove it. One day, you'll wake up responding differently, feeling differently, and you'll realize that an area has been addressed and healed.

Therapy, the altar, and deeper seeking of the Lord all play a part in our transformation. It's important to do our part and actively engage in becoming more like Him. The worst part about the forgotten is that you don't realize what hasn't been addressed until it shows up at the most inconvenient time. Just as takeoff is about to happen, something unexpected can arise. Has life made you forget who you are and who God created you to be? Sometimes, words spoken through conversations with others can shape the core of who you are. We can fall into the trap of thinking that everyone else is moving ahead while we're stuck, left behind, unsure how to move forward. We feel comfortable staying in our shell, our cocoon, and while something may have been produced during that time of seclusion, we must be mindful not to stay there.

There are times when we need to pull away from everything and everyone to see matters for what they truly are through the eyes of the Lord. But there are also times when we need to seek wise counsel to ensure that different stages and factors in our lives are addressed properly.

If you are reading this book, I want you to know that you are not forgotten. You are not being overlooked because of how uniquely God made you.

"Can a woman forget her nursing child, that she should have no compassion on the son of her womb? Even these may forget, yet I will not forget you. Behold, I have engraved you on the palms of my hands; your walls are continually before me."

— ISAIAH 49:15-16

"Do not be afraid or discouraged, for the Lord will personally go ahead of you. He will be with you; He will neither fail you nor abandon you."

— DEUTERONOMY 31:8

"You saw me before I was born. Every day of my life was recorded in your book. Every moment was laid out before a single day had passed. How precious are your thoughts about me, O God. They cannot be numbered!"

— PSALM 139:16-17

Before problems begin to arise in your life, both outwardly and inwardly, God has a word for you to address the insecurities we sometimes embrace. We don't need to be secure in ourselves; we can find security in who the Creator made us to be.

"The Lord will perfect that which concerns me."

— PSALM 138:8

"I, the Lord, made you, and I will not forget you. Always remember, you are not forgotten. Not by God. Be encouraged."

— ISAIAH 44:21

"I have loved you with an everlasting love; I have drawn you with loving-kindness."

— JEREMIAH 31:3

Be determined not to walk through life in self-pity or regret. Be determined to overcome and not succumb to what has happened. The abundant life that God has afforded us needs to be embraced, knowing that we can live in peace and love, no matter what's happening around us.

We are about to go back. This exercise is placed at the beginning of the book because it may take some time to walk through. This part of the book will set the foundation for everything that follows, so please be careful not to skip over this process.

I encourage you to pray before addressing each stage, and consider having an accountability partner to walk through this process with you. I've provided space for two pages per age span, but you may find that you need more. Extra pages are available at the back of the book for additional writing. After you have finished the age spans, say the prayer of breakthrough and release at the end. Find a scripture text that you can use to help you walk through the specific area that is being addressed.

TRAUMATIC SITUATIONS

Provide an example of a traumatic, life-changing, or difficult situation that could have occurred during your various age spans.

Start to think about these questions. There will be space to write your responses on the following page after the prayer.

1. What happened?
2. How did it make you feel?
3. How has it affected certain areas of your life?
4. Are you ready to move forward and live?
5. Release it to God and invite him to heal you.

Consider this example: I was affected by verbal abuse at six years old by my babysitter. I was afraid to tell others because I didn't want to be seen as a problem child. This experience has affected my life, as I tend to cut people off, end relationships, and slip into depression whenever I feel criticized. I am now ready to move on from this trauma and live life freely.

Say this prayer before you begin:

Dear Heavenly Father,

I come before you in this moment to release the traumatic situation that happened in my childhood. I acknowledge the pain and hurt it caused me and the impact it has had on my life. I invite you, Lord, to bring healing and restoration to every area that has been affected.

I surrender this situation to you, recognizing that I cannot carry this burden on my own. I place it in your hands, knowing that you are able to bring beauty from ashes and turn my pain into purpose.
I declare that I am ready to move forward in my life, leaving behind the shackles of the past. I choose to forgive those who have hurt me, releasing any resentment and bitterness. I ask for your grace and strength to walk in forgiveness and love.

I invite you, Holy Spirit, to guide me through this healing process. I ask for wisdom and discernment to navigate any triggers or emotions that may arise. Help me to be honest and vulnerable with myself and with trusted individuals who can offer support and accountability.

As I address each stage of my life, I pray for your presence and guidance. May your love and healing touch every area that has been affected by the traumatic situation. Help me to see myself through your eyes, with a renewed sense of worth and purpose.

I seek your Word, Lord, to find comfort and encouragement throughout this journey. Please lead me to the scriptures that can bring healing and transformation to the specific areas that need addressing.

Thank you, Lord, for your faithfulness and unfailing love. I trust in your ability to heal and restore. I surrender this journey to you, knowing that you will bring breakthrough and wholeness.

In Jesus' name, I pray,
Amen.

Now that we've prayed, let's revisit the aforementioned questions. Please record your responses to each question below:

1. What traumatic, life-changing, or difficult event took place?

_____

_____

_____

_____

_____

_____

_____

_____

2. How did it make you feel?

_____
_____
_____
_____
_____
_____
_____
_____
_____

3. How has it affected certain areas of your life?

_____
_____
_____
_____
_____
_____
_____
_____
_____

4. Are you ready to move forward and live?

_____
_____
_____
_____
_____
_____
_____
_____
_____

5. Release it to God and invite him to heal you. Write down what God reveals to you.

_____

_____

_____

_____

_____

_____

_____

_____

_____

Release and Invite:

I, ___(your name)___ release the ___(verbal abuse)___ that resulted in me living in a life of ___fear___. God, I invite you into this situation and ask you to release me from it, according to the scripture 2 Timothy 1:7: "For God has not given us a spirit of fear, but of power and of love and of a sound mind."

I, _____ release the _____ that resulted in me living in a life of _____ . God, I invite you into to this situation and ask you to release me from it, according to the scripture _____

_____

_____

_____

_____

Child (0-12 years old):

_____
_____
_____
_____
_____
_____
_____
_____
_____
_____
_____
_____
_____
_____

Adolescent (13-17 years old):

_____
_____
_____
_____
_____
_____
_____
_____
_____
_____
_____
_____
_____
_____

Teenager (13-19 years old):

_____

_____

_____

_____

_____

_____

_____

_____

_____

_____

_____

_____

_____

_____

Young Adult (18-30 years old):

_____

_____

_____

_____

_____

_____

_____

_____

_____

_____

_____

_____

_____

_____

Middle-Aged Adult (40-65 years old):

_____

_____

_____

_____

_____

_____

_____

_____

_____

_____

_____

_____

_____

_____

Senior (65 years old and above):

_____

_____

_____

_____

_____

_____

_____

_____

_____

_____

_____

_____

_____

_____

INTERACTIVE ACTIVITY

Please take some time to reflect on any unresolved traumas or unfulfilled dreams and visions in your life that may be crying out for attention. How have they affected you, and what steps can you take to address and heal from them?

_____

_____

_____

_____

_____

_____

_____

_____

_____

_____

_____

_____

_____

_____

_____

_____

_____

_____

_____

_____

_____

_____

_____

_____

_____

_____

_____

_____

Read through the passages in this chapter that discuss the various parts of ourselves that need to be aligned with God's purpose, including our hearts, souls, minds, and bodies. Reflect on how each of these areas is currently aligned with God and consider what areas may need further refinement or healing.

_____

_____

_____

_____

_____

_____

_____

_____

_____

_____

_____

_____

_____

_____

_____

_____

_____

_____

_____

_____

_____

_____

_____

_____

_____

_____

_____

_____

_____

_____

_____

_____

_____

Consider the importance of repetition in programming our subconscious minds and aligning ourselves with God's Word. What steps can you take to intentionally program your subconscious mind with God's truth and overcome any negative thought patterns or beliefs?

_____

_____

_____

_____

_____

_____

_____

_____

_____

_____

_____

_____

_____

_____

_____

_____

_____

_____

_____

_____

_____

_____

_____

_____

_____

_____

_____

_____

_____

_____

_____

_____

Consider the role of discipline in our transformation process. In what areas can you be more disciplined in seeking the Lord and actively engaging in becoming more like Him?

_____

_____

_____

_____

_____

_____

_____

_____

_____

_____

_____

_____

_____

_____

_____

_____

_____

_____

_____

_____

_____

_____

_____

_____

_____

_____

_____

_____

_____

_____

Reflect on the importance of addressing and healing from unresolved traumas and unfulfilled dreams to move forward and achieve your purpose. How can you prioritize your healing and growth in these areas to fully step into the promises that God has for you?

_____

_____

_____

_____

_____

_____

_____

_____

_____

_____

_____

_____

_____

_____

_____

_____

_____

_____

_____

_____

_____

_____

_____

_____

_____

_____

_____

_____

_____

_____

_____

2. THE BROKEN SYSTEM
I HAVE TAKEN YOU AS FAR AS YOU CAN GO

In life, we have grown accustomed to walking "systematically" broken. Have you ever considered the concept of being systematically broken and how God needs to break down the broken system that has shaped your life? We are born into a broken world, influenced by flawed traditions, family dynamics, and culture. But God desires to restore His fully established kingdom, which began with Jesus' life, death, burial, and resurrection. The Kingdom of God encompasses a belief system and a way of living that prepares us for eternity. As believers in Jesus Christ, our citizenship is no longer tied to this world; we are citizens of Heaven.

The Kingdom of God is about God's rule over our lives and the world. It's about living with humility and servanthood, and finding joy in restoring the broken. We can participate in His kingdom by acknowledging Him as our King and living as His ambassadors. As believers, we are called to live with purpose, waiting for Jesus' return and trusting that He will transform our lives and bring us wholeness. Authority comes from being obedient to God's will, and we must be willing to submit to His plan. Let's live with faith, trust in God's plan, embrace our Heavenly citizenship, and eagerly anticipate the fulfillment of His kingdom.

"But our citizenship is in heaven. And we eagerly await a Savior from there, the Lord Jesus Christ, who, by the power that enables him to bring everything under his control, will transform our lowly bodies so that they will be like his glorious body."

— PHILIPPIANS 3:20-21

But there's far more to life for us. We're citizens of high heaven! We're waiting for the arrival of the Savior, the Master, Jesus Christ, who will transform our earthly bodies into glorious bodies like His own. He'll make us beautiful and whole with the same powerful skill by which He is putting everything as it should be, under and around Him.

THE PRAYER OF SALVATION

If you are reading this and have not yet accepted Jesus Christ into your life as your personal Savior and Lord, I invite you to take a moment of personal reflection. Consider this opportunity to accept this invitation and say this prayer out loud.

"Dear God, I come to You in humility and repentance. I acknowledge that I have sinned and fallen short of Your glory. I ask for Your forgiveness and mercy. I believe that Jesus Christ is Your Son, who died on the cross for my sins and rose from the dead to give me eternal life. I invite You to come into my heart and be my Lord and Savior. I surrender my life to You and ask for Your guidance and direction. Thank You for saving me and giving me eternal life."

If you have said this prayer, then you are saved. You will be preserved until the day of your redemption, and your eternity will be spent in heaven with your Savior and Lord, Jesus Christ. I encourage you to find a local church, connect with it, attend faithfully, and serve as God leads you. Be discipled into the Kingdom of God.

THE BROKEN GOVERNMENT (KINGDOM OF DARKNESS)

The current system is designed to break and destroy us. It is not set up for us to succeed. We must be broken in order to be rebuilt as God originally intended. We often find ourselves functioning in a broken state, trying to hold things together as they crumble around us. In Colossians 1:13, the apostle Paul describes salvation as God's act of rescuing believers from the dominion of darkness and transferring them into the Kingdom of His beloved Son. This imagery of rescue and deliverance, from darkness to light, can be seen throughout the book of Isaiah, and Paul may have drawn inspiration from it.

The "kingdom of darkness" in Colossians 1:13 is also referred to as the "domain of darkness" or the "dominion of darkness." Bible scholars interpret Paul's meaning in different ways. For some, the kingdom of darkness represents a spiritual realm where Satan holds authority and reigns over human hearts, resisting the kingdom of God and Jesus Christ. Ephesians 6:12 explains that our struggle is not against flesh and blood but against evil rulers and authorities in the dark world.

Prior to salvation, the minds of unbelievers are filled with darkness, and they are far from the life God offers. Unbelievers live under the rule of darkness, while Christians live in the light and are transformed by God's grace. When Paul encountered Jesus on the road to Damascus, Jesus spoke of sending him as a servant to open people's eyes, turning them from darkness to light, from the power of Satan to God. This transformation brings forgiveness and a place among God's people, set apart by faith in Christ. The kingdom of darkness is a realm marked by sin and rebellion toward God, contrasting with the kingdom of Christ, which becomes the new home of believers. Through salvation, we are relocated from our old lives and become citizens of heaven and members of God's family. We are rescued from the dangerous dominion of darkness and transferred into the glorious light and fellowship of God's kingdom, where Jesus reigns. The kingdom of darkness is characterized by death. However, God, rich in mercy and love, gave us life by raising Christ from the dead. Through Jesus' sacrifice, sin's curse of death is removed, and we are set free.

We cannot be overtaken or consumed by an evil agenda sent from hell, as we know that God is with us. Jesus, as the light of the world, introduces justice by guiding us out of darkness and into the light, bringing hope to those in darkness. By receiving God's gift of salvation in Jesus, we transition from death to life. In His mercy and love, God gathers us from the bondage of sin and death in the kingdom of darkness and brings us into the eternal light and freedom of Christ's kingdom. As we stand in this justice, we realize that the root word for justice is "just," which means righteous—a reminder that God's justice is rooted in His righteousness. He wants to address the injustice in the church, saying that when His people humble themselves, pray, seek His face, and turn from their wicked ways, He will forgive our sins and heal the land.

> *"Therefore judge nothing before the appointed time; wait until the Lord comes. He will bring to light what is hidden in darkness and will expose the motives of the heart. At that time each will receive their praise from God."*
>
> — 1 CORINTHIANS 4:5

> *"I tell you, he will see that they get justice, and quickly. However, when the Son of Man comes, will he find faith on the earth?"*
>
> — LUKE 18:8

> *"Because of the increase of wickedness, the love of most will grow cold, but the one who stands firm to the end will be saved."*
>
> — MATTHEW 24:12-13

The world's system is full of corruption, and we know it operates in evil, as many have chosen their master, the prince of the air. We must remember that we are born in sin and shaped in iniquity. This is why it is so important to intercede for the injustice in the world, but the Lord told me to start with the church, to ensure that we are holding up our end of the bargain. Instead of merely having church, we must be the church.

"Thy Kingdom come, thy will be done on earth as it is in Heaven."

— MATTHEW 6:10

The Kingdom of God is *rooted in justice.* It is established and supported by justice, and justice is the natural overflow of a life redeemed by Christ and filled with the Holy Spirit. The justice that Jesus gives us, and that we, in turn, are called to release, is victorious, transformational, and restorative. We are to be examples of justice, order, and righteousness. In Greek, justice means virtue, standards, and excellence. Does the church at large exemplify these attributes?

"But we have this treasure in earthen vessels, that the excellence of the power may be of God and not of us."

— 2 CORINTHIANS 4:7

Transformation happens internally through the power of the Holy Spirit, not by our own efforts. To make a distinction, the term "justice" is typically associated with judgments or decisions that set things right, while "righteousness" refers to personal involvement in addressing injustices and responding to the needs within those parameters.

"But I tell you, love your enemies and pray for those who persecute you, that you may be children of your Father in heaven."

— MATTHEW 5:43-48

"When justice is done, it brings joy to the righteous but terror to evildoers."

— PROVERBS 21:15

"Do not take revenge, my dear friends, but leave room for God's wrath, for it is written: "It is mine to avenge; I will repay," says the Lord."

— ROMANS 12:19

We cannot be overtaken or consumed by an evil agenda sent from hell, for we know that God is with us. Like Habakkuk, we may have questions and not fully understand, but we can still say, "I will stand my watch and wait to see what the Lord will say." Even as we stand, instructions come from the Lord, guiding us. The land will be healed, souls will be saved, and people will be restored when we, as a people, repent so that we can hear His voice. We are walking in injustice because we are not attentive to His ways, and the sin of disobedience is the root issue. We are doing church our own way and not seeing results, because we do not need to prove anything to each other but rather a gospel to defend.

"For it is time for judgment to begin with God's household; and if it begins with us, what will the outcome be for those who do not obey the gospel of God?"

— 1 PETER 4:17

The Bible offers several teachings on justice among believers in Christ. Justice within the body of Christ is grounded in discernment, accountability, forgiveness, love, and restitution.

1. *Discernment and Accountability*: In Matthew 18:15-17, Jesus teaches that if a brother or sister in Christ sins against us, we are to approach them privately and try to reconcile. If they refuse to listen, we are to bring one or two others to talk with them. If they still refuse to listen, we are to bring it before the church for accountability.

2. *Forgiveness*: In Colossians 3:13, Paul teaches that we should bear with one another and forgive one another if we have a

grievance against someone. Just as the Lord has forgiven us, we should also forgive one another.

3. *Loving One Another:* In 1 John 4:20-21, John teaches that if anyone says they love God but hates their brother or sister in Christ, they are a liar. We are called to love one another because God first loved us.

4. *Restitution*: In Luke 19:8-9, Zacchaeus the tax collector repented of his wrongdoing by promising to repay those he had cheated four times over. Restitution is a way to make things right with others and seek forgiveness and reconciliation.

BREAKING FOR A PURPOSE

God breaks us to build us. He takes us from a place of brokenness to a place of establishment in His kingdom. There are no loopholes or cracks in this fully established system. The enemy cannot enter because he is already defeated. To fulfill our role as Kingdom citizens, we must address our brokenness. We must not abandon our posts, even when challenges arise. God has authorized us to take dominion and walk in our God-given authority, but we need to overcome our state of brokenness.

When I think about brokenness, I think of the woman with the alabaster box who took her expensive oil and anointed the feet of Jesus. I consider the oil and the olives that are crushed to produce it. The crushing process is not gentle at all. It is a continuous process, ensuring that all of the oil is extracted from the olive. Once the oil is produced, it can be used for various purposes. The people who crushed the olives and produced the oil that the woman used to anoint Jesus' feet did not know the significance of their work. This teaches us about the process of our lives. We don't always know what will happen from A to Z or what it will lead to, but ultimately, it will have an impact on someone else. That's what purpose is all about. What God has called each of us to do on earth is for a purpose. We go to school to gain knowledge, and as the

Bible says, our gifts will make room for us and bring us before great men.

"So there's a nurturing in the training that happens both academically and spiritually, that gets us to where we need to be where our purpose is fulfilled effectively."

— PROVERBS 18:16

BROKENNESS AS A QUALIFICATION

To fully understand our role as believers and how to live in alignment with God's will, we must first recognize the importance of brokenness. The broken parts of ourselves—the aspects that are not surrendered to God—cannot grant us entry into the fullness of what He has for us. As a result, we often experience only partial blessings, as we are only partially living according to God's ways. When we consider what it means to be a totally yielded son or daughter of God, we see that it requires a state of brokenness. The question, "What does a totally yielded son or daughter look like?" becomes a constant inquiry in our lives. We must ascend to a higher level and remain in that ascended state. However, ascension is only possible through brokenness. As the Psalmist writes in Psalm 51:17, "The sacrifices of God are a broken spirit; a broken and contrite heart, O God, you will not despise." It is worth noting that the word "contrite" can be understood as 'repentant,' while 'heart' refers to our very core.

THE BROKEN HEART

Romans 10:8-9 explains that a repentant heart is necessary for salvation. To be broken, we must separate our will from God's will. Every access point in our lives requires brokenness. Romans further emphasizes that our salvation is linked to what we believe in our hearts. Therefore, for our spirits to be broken, we must fully submit ourselves to the Holy Spirit, allowing our will to align with God's will. A few synonyms for separation are blows, shocks, or strains. This separation is necessary at each access point in our lives. We ourselves are the access points through which God wants to work. Brokenness involves breaking to build, crushing to produce, and breaking off to add something new. Just like a wireless access point, we enable the connection between the spiritual and physical worlds, allowing God's power to flow through us.

When faced with a challenging situation, it is easy to play the victim or succumb to self-pity. When this was my reality, God gently whispered, "Take this one." He urged me to avoid prolonged mourning—not by ignoring the pain, but by assuring me that He would address and heal my wounds—for He breaks us to build us up. Instead of praying for a way out of the brokenness, we must recognize that the broken place is the way in. God needs the raw materials of our brokenness to construct a solid foundation within us. God is our wall of protection.

In Ephesians 2:17-22, the Body of Christ is described as the walls of a temple, "built on the foundation of the apostles and prophets, with Christ Jesus Himself as the cornerstone." We are all part of the wall that "grows into a holy sanctuary in the Lord."

"Whoever has no rule over his own spirit Is like a city broken down, without walls."

— PROVERBS 25:28

The wall represents establishment and order in our lives. Jesus Christ shoulders the responsibility of government, and our task is to walk out and establish His law.

"For to us a child is born, to us a son is given, and the *government will be on his shoulders. And he will be called Wonderful Counselor, Mighty God, Everlasting Father, Prince of Peace.*"

— ISAIAH 9:6

We were born into a broken kingdom, consistently experiencing brokenness and destruction. But even in our brokenness, God can turn what the enemy meant for evil into something good. Through being born again, we enter into a new government, fully established and intact. No longer are we held together by broken pieces; in God's Kingdom, there are no loopholes, no cracks in our vessel, and no way for the enemy to track us. As we embrace our brokenness, we realize that it has a purpose— it cannot last forever.

UNVEILING THE HEART

In Romans 8, the questions are posed: "Who shall separate us from the love of Christ? Shall trouble or hardship or persecution or famine or nakedness or danger or sword?" As it is written: "For your sake we face death all day long; we are considered as sheep to be slaughtered."

The reference to Pharaoh as a tool of God's power is highlighted. The verses speak to the mercy and hardening of individuals as chosen by God for His purposes. The analogy of the potter and clay emphasizes God's right to shape His creation as He sees fit.

Have you ever been in a situation in any relationship— whether with your supervisor, close friend, spouse, or child—where you ask yourself, "Why is this conflict here? Why am I being misunderstood?" The simplicity of the issue should not have been magnified to this degree. You have to be discerning to understand when there is spiritual warfare and something is trying to come between relationships that God ordained to be. Sometimes, even when we've done all we can to resolve conflicts through wise counsel and prayer, and have compromised as much as possible, it's still not enough to bring about recovery. In those situations, we must release the issue to God and surrender our control. We must say, "This is your life, not mine. I don't want to be in charge; I want you to guide me." We must trust that God will bring about the right outcomes for our lives, even if it means releasing someone who is not meant to be part of our journey.

Reflecting on personal experiences, one might ask how things unfolded as they did. Despite intentional planning, unexpected storms can alter the course. In the current climate, where evil is blatant, there is a reluctance in the body of Christ to stand firm for fear of offending. However, true judgment is an act of love, bringing order and righteousness.

The heart is the core that drives life, and its condition speaks volumes. With a call from God for a clean heart, the need for transformation and a new spirit is imperative. It is through this renewal that the Spirit of God can dwell within, bringing about spiritual change. Looking at the role of the heart in belief, the importance of a sincere heart is acknowledged in the process of salvation. The Spirit plays a crucial role, drawing individuals toward faith and enabling them to believe in the truth. These concepts are foundational and significant in understanding the spiritual journey and the transformation that occurs within the heart.

Your Readiness to Ascend

Ascending to the holy hill means standing firm under pressure, persecution, and betrayal. Dealing with our brokenness unlocks the power of God within us. Through our brokenness, we become vessels fit for His use, fully established and empowered to carry out His purposes.

To fully embrace our roles as believers, it is important to understand the significance of brokenness. It is only through our brokenness that we are authorized to ascend. Those who stand guard are the ones who can see ahead, prepare to help others, and sound the alarm as prophetic vessels, warning others to be on guard at all times. As children of God, we live in two dimensions: in heaven and on earth.

"Even when we were dead in sins, hath quickened us together with Christ, (by grace ye are saved;) And hath raised us up together, and made us sit together in heavenly places in Christ Jesus."

— Ephesians 2:5-6

"For we are strangers before you and sojourners, as all our fathers were. Our days on the earth are like a shadow, and there is no abiding."

— 1 CHRONICLES 29:15

"Set your affection on things above, not on things on the earth."

— COLOSSIANS 3:2

When you are seated in your heavenly place and have ascended to the holy hill of the Lord, you understand that you cannot live solely in this earthly dimension. The Bible says we walk in the Spirit so that we don't fulfill the lust of the flesh. You can't dwell in this dimension; you must live from your heavenly place. When you view life from a heavenly perspective, nothing appears as it seems, and nothing is as it is. Let's take a close look at Jeremiah's call and how the Lord trained his eyes to see.

THE CALL OF JEREMIAH

Jeremiah 1:4-19

⁴ The word of the Lord came to me, saying,
⁵ "Before I formed you in the womb I knew you, before you were born I set you apart; I appointed you as a prophet to the nations."
⁶ "Alas, Sovereign Lord," I said, "I do not know how to speak; I am too young."
⁷ But the Lord said to me, "Do not say, 'I am too young.' You must go to everyone I send you to and say whatever I command you.
⁸ Do not be afraid of them, for I am with you and will rescueyou," declares the Lord.
⁹ Then the Lord reached out his hand and touched my mouth and said to me, "I have put my words in your mouth.
¹⁰ See, today I appoint you over nations and kingdoms to uproot and tear down, to destroy and overthrow, to build and to plant."

¹¹ The word of the Lord came to me: "What do you see, Jeremiah?"

"I see the branch of an almond tree," I replied.

¹² The Lord said to me, "You have seen correctly, for I am watching to see that my word is fulfilled."

¹³ The word of the Lord came to me again: "What do you see?"

"I see a pot that is boiling," I answered. "It is tilting toward us from the north."

¹⁴ The Lord said to me, "From the north disaster will be poured out on all who live in the land.

¹⁵ I am about to summon all the peoples of the northern kingdoms," declares the Lord. "Their kings will come and set up their thrones in the entrance of the gates of Jerusalem; they will come against all her surrounding walls and against all the towns of Judah.

¹⁶ I will pronounce my judgments on my people because of their wickedness in forsaking me, in burning incense to other gods and in worshiping what their hands have made.

¹⁷ "Get yourself ready! Stand up and say to them whatever I command you. Do not be terrified by them, or I will terrify you before them.

¹⁸ Today I have made you a fortified city, an iron pillar and a bronze wall to stand against the whole land—against the kings of Judah, its officials, its priests and the people of the land.

¹⁹ They will fight against you but will not overcome you, for I am with you and will rescue you," declares the Lord.

God is training our eyes to see what He sees, and when we do, we can do what He does because we sit where He sits— in the heavenly realm. We don't go in and out; rather, we remain there. We stay there so we don't miss anything He's trying to reveal to us. We can see over and through it, leaving no loopholes for the enemy to creep in, because there will be things hidden. God called Jeremiah to speak for Him, but He had to bring him up to where He is in order for him to receive the revelation of the message he was to release. We can't understand it with our own knowledge, and we can't do it in our own strength.

According to Psalm 24, the progression of ascending to the mountain of the Lord involves being broken. Ascending into the mountain of the Lord requires us to leave behind our mistakes and the weight that ties us to our sins. We cannot carry that weight to the mountain. We need to be pure and clean in order to fulfill our roles.

Ascending requires us to push beyond the familiar into the unfamiliar and the unknown. We must discard the old and embrace the new, which involves breaking down the dried pottery and rebuilding it into something new. God molds us into who we need to be in different seasons, ensuring that we are fully equipped with new tools and a new perspective for every assignment. Being at the access point of a breakthrough, in the presence of God and on the altar, is a privilege that cannot be taken for granted. It requires us to come to the end of ourselves, to humble ourselves, and to rely entirely on God's grace.

Brokenness is a prerequisite for ascending, and it requires continuous attention and renewal. However, if we allow God to break us down, to mold and make us for every season, we will be ready to ascend to new heights and establish His Kingdom. Yes, every season of our lives requires preparation. The devil is coming for deep things, but God says that He will take the pain and address brokenness. The enemy of our souls does not want us to come into the full knowledge of who we are and who our Father is through His son, Jesus Christ. Jesus bore our brokenness on the cross so that we may live in freedom. When we break away from sin, God covers and washes away the evidence with His blood, and we are no longer tied to our sins. Brokenness must be continually addressed to prevent the enemy from gaining entry.

As we look at the establishment of the temple in the Old Testament, let's go through the process of the temple: we need to go through the altar of sacrifice, the brazen laver, and then enter the holy place, to the Holy of Holies. We cannot be washed, cleansed, or purified without first sacrificing ourselves to God. Our consecration prepares us for the new level of brokenness, and being broken is necessary for God to mold and make us for the next place.

THE TABERNACLE STRUCTURE AND ACCESS POINTS

The structure of the Tabernacle provides insight into the importance of access points that God has given us in the spiritual realm.

The altar of sacrifice is a raised platform or table where animals or offerings were sacrificed to God as a form of atonement for sins or to show devotion. This is the place where everything that pertains to us dies, and this is the point where everything that God has ordained for us to do, be, and walk in can take over. Are you ready to walk into a new life, totally different, taking off the old garment and putting on a new one—new and improved, ready to forsake all for what's next?

The brazen laver is a large basin or bowl filled with water used by priests for ritual purification before entering the sanctuary or performing sacrifices. After you have surrendered everything to God, He will begin to purify and sanctify, washing you clean daily. As we seek the Lord, pray, study the Word, and meditate on it day and night, we will see transformation happen right before our eyes—things we could not do in our own strength. God will supernaturally shift us into another realm of glory; it will no longer be a struggle, and we won't want to stay in the same place we were before.

The sanctuary, or tent of meeting, is the central place of worship and communication with God for the Israelites during their time in the wilderness. It housed the Holy of Holies and the Holy Place.

The Holy Place is the outer chamber of the sanctuary where priests performed various rituals and offered incense and showbread. It was also where the golden lampstand provided light. This is a place of worship where we acknowledge God in His sovereignty, coming before Him as we offer incense and worship daily. It is here that He brings illumination to us, providing understanding of who He is and what He has created us to be in Him. This is where a greater level of gratitude and intimacy develops, and we recognize where our help and provision come from. It moves us out of the picture, making Him the focal point.

The Holy of Holies is the innermost chamber of the sanctuary, separated by a veil, where the Ark of the Covenant was kept. It was considered the most sacred space and symbolized the presence of God. This is the most sacred place in the presence of the Lord God, where divine insight comes, and where His law, written on the tablets of our hearts, is established. This is the place where we see Him, experience Him, and encounter His presence—a one-on-one, personal encounter with our Father. This is where we come to be transformed and changed forever. Once we enter this place, everything about our lives shifts in a new direction. It is here that clear understanding is brought to situations we have struggled with for years. This is the secret place, where you come away with the Father, close the door, and receive from Him. *"You have gone as far as you can go."*

BROKENNESS AND BUILDING

Brokenness is necessary for building. The unauthorized parts of us cannot gain entry into the next place. We may be partially doing things God's way, but we need to fully yield ourselves to Him. A daughter or son who is yielded to God looks like someone who lives for Him every day.

God prompted me to write this book because of the above state-ment: "You have gone as far as you can go." Do you know that when it's time to move forward to the next place in your life, where you are will no longer satisfy you? Where you have produced the fruit that it was supposed to produce. When you don't move at the proper time, you will begin to see how frustration can easily set in. Progression is not a bad thing; it's important that when it's time to transition, you do it. Whether smooth or difficult, God's timing is key. Moving in the wrong timing can cause turbulence in your movement and arrival at the next place.

Jesus promised us, "whoever believes in Him should not perish, but have everlasting life." How will God fulfill this word? God fulfilled His word when He raised Jesus back to life—in Jesus, all of God's promises are met (2 Corinthians 1:20). We are saved by His life. What is fulfill-ment to you, and how does that look in your life?

> "Enlarge the site of your tent, and let your tent curtains be stretched out; do not hold back; lengthen your ropes, and drive your pegs deep."
>
> — ISAIAH 54:2

Enlarge, in Hebrew, means to increase, amplify, enhance, augment, magnify. The verb לרבות translates to multiply, increase, become great, and grow.

However, I cannot enlarge what needs to be done away with. The building has to crumble; it must come down to nothing. Only after the dust settles and the rubbish is cleared can you build the foundation and rebuild again. Your intellectual capabilities can only take you so far. You have covered ground, learned, practiced, mastered, achieved triumphs, and made mistakes. You have listened, conformed, and disobeyed. So, this next place will require obedience without compromise.

CUTTING LOOSE TIES TO SOAR: EMBRACING GOD'S PLAN FOR PROGRESS AND TRANSFORMATION

From one year to the next, we have made progress in various areas of our lives. Yet, there may be a lingering feeling that we could have done more or positioned ourselves differently for even greater accomplishments. Our response to adversity now will shape the pages of history and become a blueprint for the next generation. The question is, will we crash and burn or soar and conquer? God is urging us to cut loose the emotional ties that hold us back so that we may truly soar in our purpose and destiny. We cannot soar while being connected to emotional strings, unresolved relationships, or limiting connections.

DRY LAND

"I'm taking you out of muddy waters onto dry land." These words are a promise of transformation and renewal. They remind us that God is a God of change and restoration, capable of taking us from a place of darkness and confusion to a place of light and clarity. In the Word of God, we find numerous examples of God bringing people out of difficult circumstances. He rescued the Israelites from slavery in Egypt, parted the Red Sea, and provided for their needs in the wilderness. He did the same for the prophet Ezekiel, who was called to speak to the Israelites about their rebellion against God.

In Ezekiel 34:18-19, God asks Ezekiel, "Must you make the rest of the water muddy with your feet?" The question is rhetorical and highlights the tendency of humans to pollute things that are good and pure. We often take what is meant to nourish and sustain us, like clear water, and muddy it with our selfish desires and actions. But God is greater than our mistakes. He can take us out of the muddy waters and onto dry land. He is able to transform our lives and bring us into a new era of peace and prosperity. This transformation is not just about external circumstances but also about internal change. It is about being renewed in our minds and hearts and being made new creations in Christ. As we look to God for this transformation, we can trust that He will be faithful to complete what He has started. He will take us out of the muddy waters and into a new life, where we can live in freedom and joy.

Proverbs 25:25-27 reminds us that "like cold water to a weary soul is good news from a distant land." Receive this word for yourself: God is preparing to send you good news from afar. This may come from an unexpected place, but it will be crucial for your full progression. The divine revelation that God is about to bring into your life will be a source of refreshment and renewal for your mind, enabling you to conceive what God is trying to impart to you and accomplish through you. However, those who give way to the wicked are compared to "a muddied spring or a polluted well." This verse serves as a warning against compromising our values and principles to fit in with others.

God is saying to us today, "I'm taking you out of muddy waters onto dry land." This is not just a promise but a reality. It is a promise that He is capable of taking us out of our current circumstances and into a new life, where we can live in freedom and joy. We can trust that He will complete what He has started and that He will guide us through the process of transformation.

We must be willing to surrender our old ways and receive new life from God. It's time to let go of our past mistakes and receive God's forgiveness. We must trust in His goodness and faithfulness, even when we don't understand what He is doing. In the end, God's promise is one of hope and renewal. He is taking us out of muddy waters onto dry land and into a new life where we can live in freedom and joy. Will you receive this promise today?

WE ARE IN AN ERA OF GREATNESS

God's plan for His children in this era is greater than we can imagine, and it will be impactful. We must grasp the magnitude of what lies ahead and align our actions accordingly. By acknowledging the challenges we face every day and walking in the authority of Christ, we will inspire the next generation to rise above adversity. What will the next generation testify about concerning what happened in this era? We do this by grasping the Next Generation's Narrative. Our actions now will speak volumes later. We must delve into the impact our actions have on the narrative that the next generation will remember. By responding to adversity with strength, resilience, and unwavering faith in God, we leave a powerful legacy. The life we live today is writing our history. Our lives serve as a template for the next generation. By examining the history-making actions of those who came before us, we gain insight into how our responses can shape the course of history.

With our submission to Him, God is cutting loose ties for true soaring. God is urging us to let go of the need to control everything. Some things are meant to be without our intervention. By surrendering our desire to control outcomes, we can soar to new heights in alignment with God's plan. When we embrace our purpose, the essence of who we are is released. True soaring occurs when we step into our calling and do what we were born to do. By aligning our actions with our purpose, we unlock new levels of fulfillment and impact.

THE WORLD IS WAITING FOR THE TRANSFORMED YOU— WILL YOU SHOW UP?

Embracing transformation is the key to each season of our lives. Just as a tree planted by rivers of water brings forth fruit in its season, we too can flourish as we align ourselves with God's plan. This chapter provides practical guidance on embracing transformation and producing fruit. Our actions now will go down in history. God is reminding us to be sober-minded. We should not force something that was not meant to be.

Therefore, God is providing you with fresh soil, new opportunities.

With new soil comes new seed, being planted in a new place. Your elevation occurs when you embrace the endless possibilities of God for your
life. Every seed planted in the previous season served its purpose, and
now you can fully embrace the new. God rewards those who diligently
seek Him, and as you ascend to higher heights, you will see and hear
clearly to know what to do differently.

The transformed you is emerging. Every season should bring
about a transformation within you. As described in Psalm 1:1-3, the
one who delights in the law of the Lord is like a tree planted by
streams of water, bearing fruit in its season and prospering in all
endeavors. As Ecclesiastes 3:1 reminds us, there is a time and season
for everything under heaven. When will it be your time? He is saying
the time is now! Say it so that you and the world can hear it: "The
time is now!"

THE MULTIPLICITY OF GOD: LESSONS FROM EAGLES

The Purposeful Creation:

Let's take a moment to examine the eagle. We recognize that everything
God created serves a purpose. Eagles symbolize strength, wisdom, and
grace, all of which hold valuable lessons for our spiritual journey.

Unity and Sharing Information:

In the kingdom of eagles, unity is essential for survival. These remarkable creatures come together to share information, rely on each other for
guidance, and defend their territories. Similarly, believers are called to
embrace unity, support one another, and share knowledge to enhance
their spiritual growth.

Alone But Soaring:

Eagles are solitary creatures, choosing to fly alone and at high altitudes.
This peculiarity reminds us of the importance of distancing ourselves
from negative influences and distractions. Just as eagles don't fly with

sparrows, we must not allow ourselves to be entangled with those who hinder our spiritual progress.

Embracing Fresh Prey:

The dietary habits of eagles teach us the significance of letting go of the dead things in our lives. Eagles only feast on fresh prey, symbolizing the need to release the burdens of the past and embrace new opportunities aligned with God's purposes. Dwelling on past mistakes and grievances hinders our spiritual growth and prevents us from soaring to new heights.

A Vision Beyond Obstacles:

Eagles possess remarkable vision and remain focused on their targets, regardless of the obstacles in their path. As believers, we are encouraged to cultivate a clear spiritual vision and remain unwavering in our pursuit of God's purposes. No matter the challenges we face, maintaining focus will allow us to overcome and soar above them.

Finding Strength in the Storm:

Eagles find excitement and strength in the midst of storms. They use the winds generated by the storm to lift themselves higher, above the clouds. Similarly, believers should not fear the storms of life but instead find solace in knowing that adversity can propel us to greater spiritual heights. It is in the storms that we learn to rely on God's strength and experience growth.

Stepping Out of Comfort Zones:

Eagles teach us that growth and transformation require stepping out of our comfort zones. Just as they remove soft grass and feathers from their nests to make their young uncomfortable, we must be willing to leave behind familiarity, complacency, and stagnant situations to experience true spiritual growth.

Renewal and Growth:

As eagles age, they undergo a transformative process called molting. They retreat to a remote location, painfully shed their old feathers, and break their beaks and claws against rocks to ensure complete renewal. This process, though painful, allows them to emerge stronger and more powerful than before. Likewise, believers are called to undergo spiritual renewal, shedding old habits and breaking free from the limitations of the past to experience true growth and transformation.

As we explore the multiplicity of God through the wisdom and symbolism of eagles, we find that these magnificent creatures offer profound lessons about unity, distancing ourselves from negativity, embracing fresh opportunities, maintaining focus, finding strength in the storms, stepping out of comfort zones, and undergoing renewal and growth. By embracing these lessons, we can soar to new heights in our relationship with God and fulfill our true potential. May the wisdom we have learned from eagles guide us as we strive to embrace the multiplicity and purposefulness of God.

> *"But those who wait on the Lord shall renew their strength; They shall mount up with wings like eagles, They shall run and not be weary, They shall walk and not faint."*
>
> — ISAIAH 40:31

When you have reached your capacity where you are, when you have gone as far as you can on this level, when you have exhausted every aspect of this playing field, you come back to the table and seek for more, for the next, for the new.

* * *

Based on the information that you have read above, answer this question on the following page.

When you have reached your peak and there is nowhere else for you to go, what do you do?

_____

_____

_____

_____

_____

_____

_____

_____

_____

_____

_____

DEMAND ON THE REMNANT

In these times, there is a demand on the remnant. Romans 9:27 states, "Though the number of the Israelites be like the sand by the sea, only the remnant will be saved."

What is being exposed now was happening all along. Nothing that is covered up will remain hidden; it is time for everything to be revealed. We need to be prepared for what is coming. Judgment has hit the earth, and we must be ready. The final exam before elevation is approaching, and the test will determine if we make it to the next level. Judgment brings discipline, but it also brings reward—rewards that are based on our level of commitment to Christ. To do this, we must recognize when we have reached our peak and when it's time to progress.

Luke 12:2 tells us that everything hidden will be revealed. Isaiah 63:10 shows us the consequences of rebellion and grieving the Holy Spirit.

Jesus refers to Himself as the gate for the sheep in John 10:7-9. He is the access point to salvation and pasture. In Revelation 2:25-27, Jesus promises authority to those who conquer and keep His works until the end. He is the way to reach the end! Jesus speaks about the narrow way in Matthew 7:13-14, explaining that few find it. Many choose the wide path of self-righteousness, but the narrow path leads to life. God wants to give us a revelation about ourselves, but He must break us open first. Jesus spoke to a large crowd about how the Jewish religious leaders were leading them astray by appearing religious through visible rituals. They were using the wide gate of self-righteousness. God is doing a great humbling in the Body of Christ.

EZEKIEL'S PROPHECY AND THE ROOMS FOR PRIESTS

Ezekiel's prophecy describes a new temple and vision that stresses the purity of the place of worship. The restoration of the gates and their order determines the restoration of the kingdom's establishment. Outside the inner gate were the rooms for the singers, and the priests who had charge of the altar were the sons of Zadok. The door on the east gate was shut because God used this door to exit and enter, facing the east. This symbolizes the eternal presence of God, and Ezekiel's temple is a place of His perpetual dwelling. There is a window of opportunity for all who are willing to enter in.

Matthew 6:6 says, "But you, when you pray, go into your room, and when you have shut your door, pray to your Father who is in the secret place; and your Father who sees in secret will reward you openly." You are about to embark on a season of sacrifice; everything that you thought needed to be done away with, God will reveal so that you can release it and make room for what He is saying right now to lead you to where you need to go in the future.

It's okay to admit that the way you have operated throughout life may have been based on a broken system. It may have been centered around a broken perspective of how life is supposed to be, and that broken place has gone as far as it can take you.

Are you tired of the norm? Are you frustrated with not seeing the progress that you know your life deserves? Are you tired of seeing the people around you suffer because your progression is not where it needs to be?

There are some people who will gain strength and determination to move forward in their lives when they see you push through the things that have been holding you back. This train has no more stops; it has reached the end of its destination, and you must move forward. You can choose to stay on the train with no movement, or you can choose to get on the train that is moving in a new direction.

INTERACTIVE ACTIVITY

Reflect on the information presented in this chapter about cutting loose ties to soar, embracing transformation, and finding strength in the storms. Consider how you can apply each of these concepts to your own life.

_____
_____
_____
_____
_____
_____
_____
_____
_____

Think about a time when you felt like you had reached your peak and had nowhere else to go. What did you do? Did you continue to push forward, or did you take a step back to reevaluate your path? Write about this experience in the space below and reflect on what you learned from it.

_____
_____
_____
_____
_____
_____
_____
_____

Read Luke 12:2, Isaiah 63:10, John 10:7-9, Revelation 2:25-27, and Matthew 7:13-14. Reflect on the messages from each of these verses and how they relate to the overall theme of this chapter.

_____

_____

_____

_____

_____

_____

_____

_____

_____

_____

_____

_____

_____

Read about Ezekiel's prophecy and the rooms for priests. Reflect on what this symbolizes and how it relates to your own spiritual journey.

_____

_____

_____

_____

_____

_____

_____

_____

_____

_____

_____

_____

Take some time to pray and ask God for guidance as you continue on your journey of transformation and growth. Ask Him to reveal any emotional ties or limiting connections that are holding you back, and for the strength to cut them loose so that you may truly soar in your purpose and destiny.

_____

_____

_____

_____

_____

_____

_____

_____

_____

_____

_____

Think about a time when you felt broken in your life. What did you learn from that experience? How did God use that brokenness to build you up?

_____

_____

_____

_____

_____

_____

_____

_____

_____

_____

_____

_____

_____

Take some time to reflect on your mindset. Are there any areas where you feel like you have it all together and don't need God? How can you surrender those areas to Him and allow Him to work in them?

_____

_____

_____

_____

_____

_____

_____

_____

_____

_____

_____

_____

_____

Read through Psalm 24 and make a list of the different steps involved in ascending to the holy hill. How can you apply those steps to your own life and continue to ascend to greater heights with God?

_____

_____

_____

_____

_____

_____

_____

_____

_____

_____

_____

_____

Think about the different access points in the tabernacle structure. Why do you think access points are so important? How can you ensure that you are allowing God's glory to flow through you as an access point for others?

_____

_____

_____

_____

_____

_____

_____

_____

_____

_____

_____

Finally, take some time to reflect on the concept of brokenness as a qualification. How can you embrace your brokenness in order to become a vessel that is fit for God's use and fully established to carry out His purposes?

_____

_____

_____

_____

_____

_____

_____

_____

_____

_____

_____

_____

3. Bound to Break
Built To Capacity

At any moment, something is bound to break. But what if breaking could be a good thing? What if breaking was a process that allowed you to discover something new about yourself and your purpose? In this chapter, we'll explore the idea that breaking can be transformative. We'll look at various biblical accounts of breaking and anointing and examine why breaking free from negative patterns and mindsets is critical to achieving our true potential.

As I sat there in the quiet, feeling the weight of the world on my shoulders, the words "I need a break" echoed in my mind. But it wasn't just any break I was seeking—it was a breaking within me that needed to happen. I realized that at any moment, I was bound to break, and it was a realization that shook me to my core. The concept of being bound to break resonates deeply—a revelation that at any moment, change is inevitable, and growth is on the horizon. God is breaking us open for discovery, for growth, and for a deeper understanding of ourselves and our purpose. It's a revelation I feel compelled to share—that each of us, every situation, every circumstance, is bound to break in some way. It's in these moments of discomfort, of interruption, that true transformation occurs. The breaking is necessary for our evolution, for our journey toward wholeness. It's a process we can no longer ignore—a process that requires us to ask the tough questions and seek the answers with an open heart.

Have you ever found yourself in a place in life where you questioned everything, where reality didn't align with the promises you believed or expected? This book was birthed out of those questions. The Bible tells us to seek, and we shall find, to knock, and the door shall be opened. But how often do we let things slide, accepting what's presented to us without questioning or seeking more?

God is nudging us toward something new, but we, as a collective body, have grown complacent in our comfort. We live in a time where we're urged to move forward, to forge ahead without being fully processed. The call is to progress, to advance, yet many remain unprocessed. We seek validation and celebration, but we shy away from the discomfort of growth and change. We find solace where we are celebrated rather than where we are refined. We must be willing to endure the process, even if it means being overlooked or feeling insignificant, because it is in the process that true growth occurs. There will be a series of tests that will show us where we are and where we need to be as we continue to pursue God.

Proverbs 16:9 reminds us that man plans his way, but the LORD directs his steps. We must be willing to let go of what binds us, to be released from the old ways, and to embrace the new way of the Spirit. It is through this process of breaking open that we are made ministers of a new covenant, not tied to the restrictions of the past but free to walk in the fullness of God's plan for our lives.

But can we handle the break? Are we ready for the necessary transformation that will lead us to our next level? The break is what will bring about the "it" we've been waiting for—the breakthrough, the revelation, the new beginning. In the story of the woman who anointed Jesus in Bethany, we see powerful symbolism of humility, worship, and preparation. The profound acts of anointing Jesus' head and feet carry significant meaning, symbolizing separation, consecration, and devotion to divine purpose.

Let's break it down a little further.

We have four gospels: Matthew, Mark, Luke, and John. Each one provides a unique perspective, and all of them give us insight into the story of a woman anointing Jesus, often referred to as the "Broken Alabaster Box."

In Matthew 26 and Mark 14, both stories explain that the woman anointed Jesus' head in preparation for His burial. Anointing the head signified that He was set apart and consecrated for a divine purpose, symbolizing God's approval of Him as the King of Kings and Lord of Lords, even though He would later be mocked with a crown of thorns. Similarly, in John 12 and Mark, the feet were anointed for burial, emphasizing the significance and intentionality of the act. In Luke's account, a sinful woman anointed Jesus' feet, and He proclaimed that what she had done would be remembered wherever the Gospel was preached. She had given Him everything, breaking not only her alabaster jar but also her alabaster heart.

In Jewish tradition, it was customary for a family to purchase an alabaster box filled with costly ointments and oils for their daughter as she prepared to marry. The size and weight of the box symbolized the dowry to be given for the marriage. When a man came seeking the girl's hand in marriage, she would break open the alabaster box at his feet and anoint them with the oil, signifying her commitment to him. Did the woman know that her great intention was to be broken before God, symbolizing a marriage to Christ? She could have saved this oil for marriage or other purposes, but when she knew where Jesus was, she didn't come empty-handed. She came with a box of oil more valuable than anything she ever had, and she left with more value than she could have ever imagined.

Alabaster was a hard stone, symbolizing the act of humbling oneself and breaking a hardened heart before the Lord. When filled, the alabaster jar held great worth, equivalent to thousands of dollars. God emphasized that when filled with His presence, the value of the alabaster jar increased significantly. The baptism of Jesus represented humanity and divinity without sin, humbling and showing us the process of how we should walk in the strength and power of God triumphantly, showing us that Jesus had a process of going through the normalities of life while still being the Savior of the world.

Sometimes, we feel as though we need a break from life. But God is saying to us that we need a *breaking*—it has to happen to receive all that God has for us. The *break* is what's going to cause *it to happen*. I want you to declare: *"I need a breaking in me."*

- A breaking away of the baggage
- A break from the noise
- A break from some people, places, and things

This isn't something that's easily achieved because everything that once was can't be anymore. The familiar will look and feel strange. This breaking will bring about something you have been praying for years. Some of the breaks God is trying to achieve in our lives are linked to and tied to so much; the roots are deep. The break this time will take more than the norm. This will require more than what was expected or needed in prior seasons.

The term 'bound' can be defined in various ways: it can refer to being tied, chained, or in bondage, implying a sense of restriction or captivity. Alternatively, it can mean being predestined or guaranteed to win, suggesting a sense of triumph or achievement. Spiritually bound can also mean being obligated, obliged, or duty-bound to fulfill a particular role or purpose, such as preaching and teaching the gospel to those who are lost and need uplifting. Bound can also imply being linked with or connected to something greater, serving as a destiny stopper or helper. Meanwhile, the verb "spring" means to walk or run with leaping strides, jump, or move with sudden energy and enthusiasm.

When you break free from the negatives, the positives come. The positives are there even when the negatives are present, but you can't see them because you're so bound by the effects of your past. You are bound to break the chains of stagnation. Stagnation can be your greatest enemy. Knowing our purpose is good, but preparing and walking in it in God's timing can be challenging when we are not yielded.

The Formula for Fulfilling God's Purpose for Your Life in His Timing:

1. Prayer
2. Fasting
3. Personal study of the Word of God
4. Training
5. Wise counsel
6. Connecting to people for where you are going

Many of us have been praying for more:

1. More of God
2. More patience
3. More endurance

In order for the more to happen, the broken patterns have to *stop*! What happens if 'the more' comes and you don't have the storage for it? What happens when 'the more' comes and you don't have the capacity for it? All this time, you've been saying, "Lord, I'm ready," but when "ready" shows up at your door, you say, "Wait, I'm not ready." How can this be? That's because there is something broken that has to be fixed. There is a malfunction in the system that was there all the time but showed up when 'the more' arrived.

James 1:8 says, "A double-minded man is unstable in all of his ways."God says, "I want you to take a break so that I can repair the break." We don't deal with the problem, and it becomes bigger—what was a hill becomes a mountain. All the while, you thought that you were breaking it, but in reality, it was breaking you. Many of us have been breaking for breakthrough in our lives in different areas:

1. Mind
2. Finances
3. Marriage
4. Children
5. Ministry

...and the list goes on!

STAGES OF BROKENNESS

Sometimes God interrupts our lives and breaks us down to build us up His way for the next phase of our lives.

First Stage: The Resistance to Break
(Genesis 32:22-31)

Jacob, who was born to Isaac and Rebecca, stole the birthright and blessing from his twin brother Esau and then fled to his uncle's house. He married two wives and had twelve sons and a daughter. Jacob wrestled with God and had his name changed to Israel. The breaking happened when his name was changed to Israel. He received a revelation of who he was while being who he always was and what everyone expected of him to be.

Second Stage: The Need to Break
(Genesis 37:18-36)

Joseph, the favorite son of the patriarch Jacob, was sold into slavery in Egypt by his jealous brothers, where he eventually ended up incarcerated. After correctly interpreting the dreams of Pharaoh, however, he rose to second-in-command in Egypt and saved Egypt during a famine, along with his family. His need to break was not just for him but for nations of people.

The breaking open of:

- Spiritual gifts (dream interpretation)
- Leadership (second in command to Pharaoh)

Third Stage: The Breaking
(Mark 15:24, Luke 23:33, John 19:18, Matthew 27:35)

Jesus, the Son of God, and the second person of the Holy Trinity, was conceived by the Holy Spirit, born of a virgin named Mary, performed miracles, founded the Christian Church, and died by crucifixion as a sacrifice to achieve atonement for sin. He rose from the dead, paid for the sins of all mankind, and ascended into Heaven, from where He will return. His life and ministry are recounted in the four Gospels of the New Testament.

You are breaking out!

- Breaking out of our own way
- Breaking out of our man-made traditions
- Breaking out of our own will
- Breaking out of our old mindset

You are breaking forth!

- Breaking forth into healing
- Breaking forth into deliverance
- Breaking forth into obedience to God's will
- Breaking forth into a consecrated life
- Breaking forth into a hunger and thirst after God

It's time to break free from all limitations. The concept of being bound is prevalent, whether in bondage, predestination, obligation, or connection. But breaking free from these limitations can be empowering. It allows us to take control of our lives and move toward our true calling.

We'll examine different limitations that hold us back and look at ways we can embrace the breaking process to overcome them. We are taking leaps and bounds from broken to built to capacity. Are you willing to embrace the breaking process? Breaking can be painful and uncomfortable. It requires us to confront our own limitations and flaws. But by embracing the breaking process, we allow ourselves the opportunity to transform and achieve our true potential.

We'll look at different ways we can embrace the breaking process, such as prayer, fasting, personal study, wise counsel, and faith. It's important to find a safe and supportive community to help us through it. The actions, the devotion, the surrender all point to a breaking of old ways and a preparation for the new. Breaking free from our past, from stagnation, allows us to step into a new level of self-discovery and empowerment. This intentional breaking open is a crucial step toward embracing a future filled with healing, deliverance, and alignment with God's will.

Just as they anointed Jesus for His burial, we must be willing to break open our alabaster jar, to pour out our most precious offerings to God, and to prepare ourselves for the path ahead. Mary, the sinful woman forgiven, teaches us the power of repentance, of breaking free from our past and offering ourselves fully to Jesus. Her act of humility and devotion signals a complete surrender to the will of God, an anointing of her feet for the journey ahead. We, too, are called to break free from the chains that bind us, to break free from the patterns of the past that hinder our progress. We must break free from the resistance, the need, and the breaking itself to step into the fullness of God's plan for our lives.

In the journey of faith, restoration often requires a deliberate break from the old, an interruption of familiar patterns, and a willingness to embrace the discomfort of growth. As we break forth into new realms of healing, deliverance, and obedience, we find ourselves drawing closer to God's divine purpose set before us. The break, a moment of interruption, is essential for our progression toward the next phase. God is in the business of breaking down barriers, disrupting comfortable patterns, and facilitating growth.

The stages of brokenness—*resistance, need,* and *breaking*—are essential for our growth and transformation. Just as Jacob resisted his transformation until his name was changed, just as Joseph needed to break free from his chains to fulfill his destiny, and just as Jesus broke His body for our salvation, we must be willing to break open our hearts, our minds, and our spirits for the greater purpose God has for us.

So, as we journey through life, let us remember that we are bound to break—bound to break free from the old and embrace the new, bound to break forth into healing, deliverance, and obedience to God's will. Let us embrace the process of breaking open, for it is through our brokenness that we find true freedom and purpose in God's plan for our lives. Whether you're experiencing a season of breaking or looking to embrace the process in the future, I encourage you to take the step toward transformation and see what's possible. All things are possible to those who believe.

Brokenness is a state of being. I did not realize I needed to be broken until everything around me was broken. The life that I once knew began to crumble, and I blamed the devil, people, and situations that I thought were the root cause of the brokenness. But then I began to realize that I needed to be broken, and God used those things to help facilitate my push out of comfortability into closer intimacy with Him. Sometimes we don't see issues within ourselves when everything in our lives is going well. When things begin to fall apart, we begin to analyze what is, what's not, and what should be. But I need you to realize that you have to be careful with your analysis to make sure it is through the eyes of Jesus and not through the eyes of condemnation. There are some things in your life that you had to endure, there are some mistakes that could be avoided, and there are some that were necessary. What happened five years ago, you can't change, what transpired even last year, but you can partner with God to make sure that your future steps are in sync with His plan for your life.

So, if you want to walk through this brokenness in the right state of mind, you have to do these things:

1. *Acknowledge that you need God.* Our total dependence on God is not optional. There is no human being on earth that can live life without Him. There are many in the world who do not acknowledge Him as Lord over their lives, but that does not negate the fact that we need Him to survive in this world. A car cannot operate properly if it does not have a driver. If you turn a car on that is not computerized and let it drive itself, it won't get

very far. It will crash because it has no direction. The car has no one steering it in the right place. That's how it is when we live our lives without the leadership, authority, and power of God. It's like a plane with no pilot. It's like a child with no parent. So, I want you to take a moment to say this prayer:

Lord, I acknowledge that I need you. First, I want to take this opportunity to acknowledge you as my Lord and Savior. If I haven't already done this, I invite you to be my Savior and Lord over my life.

Say this prayer:

Lord, I acknowledge that you sent your son Jesus to die for my sins to redeem me back to my Father in heaven. I repent of my sins. I acknowledge that Jesus died, was buried, and rose on the third day, and I accept you as my Lord and Savior, Jesus Christ. For those who have already accepted Jesus as their Lord, rededicate your lives back to Him; you may not think you need to do this, but this is a fresh start for you.

Lord, I rededicate my life back to you. There are some ways that I have been operating where I have not totally allowed you to direct my path. There may even be some ways that I don't realize I've been doing things in my own strength. But today, I rededicate everything that concerns my life back to you, and I invite you to come and take total control from this day forward, in Jesus' name. Amen.

2. Commit to the process of development. Many of us are operating in a state where we are underdeveloped. We have been functioning a certain way for a certain amount of time, and it's time for us to push past that place and grow to another level. But in order for us to do that, we have to enter the new place. Development requires humility; it requires another level of everything that's in your life—prayer, fasting, studying the

Word, submitting to authority, teaching, and training. (Hebrews 13:17)

3. *Patiently wait; don't move ahead of God's timing.* Many of us have made the mistake of thinking that we can help God out by not totally waiting on Him for what to do next. We think that things are not happening fast enough for us. But when we act on our own timing instead of God's, we can make mistakes. We also have to ask ourselves if things have not changed and cycles are repeating—why is that? If you are reading this book, know that your life can be supernaturally changed forever.

My hope is that by reading this book, you will be able to embrace the process yourself.

> *"But they that wait upon the Lord shall renew their strength; they shall mount up with wings as eagles; they shall run, and not be weary; and they shall walk, and not faint."*
>
> — ISAIAH 40:31

Let us deal with the brokenness so that we can be made whole.

> *"May God himself, the God who makes everything holy and whole, make you holy and whole, put you together—spirit, soul, and body—and keep you fit for the coming of our Master, Jesus Christ. The One who called you is completely dependable. If he said it, he'll do it!"*
>
> — 1 THESSALONIANS 5:23-24

A BROKEN MIND

The concept of brokenness goes beyond just physical or emotional brokenness. Often, we find that we are broken in our mindset, thinking that we have it all together and do not need God. But God reminds us that we still need Him to maintain and balance everything out. Our broken mindset can lead us to believe we can manage life without God's guidance, but this is a dangerous path. We must remember that we need God's leadership and direction in every aspect of our lives.

A lot of times, in our own mindset, we have the ability to look at a current issue, object, person, or situation and automatically evaluate it to the core. We try to figure out what it is, how we can take part in it, and how we can get away from it. This ability to analyze is a mechanism God has given us to think things through and dive deeply into our imagination. It can be a great thing, as well as a dangerous place to be, because not everything needs that level of attention.

Before a slingshot is released, it has to be stretched back to its full capacity. It needs to be stretched to gain all the momentum necessary to thrust forward. This is what God is essentially saying to us—we have to pull back to be stretched to the greatest length in order to gain all the momentum needed to thrust us forward into the next place. Oftentimes, when we think about going back, the thought is painful for many. For some, the thought is better because life was better in some sense in the past than it is in the present. Sometimes we can mentally live in the past so much that we don't put the effort needed into our forward progress.

When we think about building, a foundation is needed. We need materials, a team, and a strategy. With a vision, we can see the possibilities, but building it out can become challenging. With prayer and wise counsel, we can effectively see in real-time what we saw in our minds and imaginations.

A BROKEN BODY

The Bible says to present our bodies as a living sacrifice, holy and acceptable unto God—this is our reasonable service (Romans 12:1). The Bible also says that our bodies are the temple of the Holy Spirit (1 Corinthians 6:19). Sometimes, we mistakenly think these scriptures pertain only to our spiritual walk with God, but our physical body is not separate from our spiritual walk. If we truly understood how God made us, we would see that all of what He created us to be is connected, and no part of that should be neglected.

Did you know that God cares about what we eat daily? What if what we eat daily affects our health? Then, of course, we can seek the Lord as to what our body needs to stay healthy. This way, we wouldn't find ourselves praying for God to heal us from diseases developed in our bodies because of what we feed them. We also need to understand that what we feed our bodies affects not just our physical health but also our minds and emotions. What we eat affects how we feel and, therefore, can sometimes determine how much time we spend with the Lord and how much we can handle in the spiritual realm when we have encounters with God.

Look at the woman with the issue of blood who touched the hem of Jesus' garment—there was virtue taken out of Jesus because of her faith. So, there's something that is depleted from us in the spiritual realm as well as the physical. Jesus was human and divine, and so are we. He had to go and spend time with the Father to recharge, just like we do. He went to sleep and rested His physical body, just like we do. He ate and fed His physical body, just like we do. How is it any different for us? We must ensure that what we take into our physical bodies affects how much we get out of this life. If our physical bodies break down, they limit us in fulfilling the call of God on our lives.

A Broken Soul

The soul is defined as the non-physical, immaterial aspect of our being, often referred to as the "inner man" or "inner self." It is the seat of our emotions, desires, and values, and it is where we experience spiritual feelings and longings.

> *"And the LORD God formed man of the dust of the ground and breathed into his nostrils the breath of life; and man became a living soul."*
>
> — GENESIS 2:7

The dust of the ground formed our body, but the breath of God formed our soul.

"That according to the riches of His glory, He may grant you to be strengthened with power through His Spirit in your inner self."

— EPHESIANS 3:16

"As the deer pants for streams of water, so my soul longs for you, my God."

— PSALM 42:1

A broken soul can occur in response to the trials, stresses, and difficulties of life. It is a God-given coping or defensive mechanism in which parts or pieces of our soul literally break off to help us deal with the trauma of a particular situation. While these fragments are very much a part of us, they have their own "personality, will, and life" and often lie hidden or buried deep within us, and we may not be aware of them. However, to find healing, these parts need to be "found" and addressed, along with the main person (or core personality).

The good news is that Jesus came to heal those who have a broken heart/ soul, according to Luke 4:18-19:

"The Spirit of the LORD is upon Me, because He has anointed Me to preach the gospel to the poor; He has sent Me to heal the brokenhearted, to proclaim liberty to the captives and recovery of sight to the blind, to set at liberty those who are oppressed; to proclaim the acceptable year of the LORD."

— LUKE 4:18-19

When we are very young, and abuse or trauma occurs in our lives, it is often too much to handle. One way for a child to cope with trauma is to disconnect or dissociate from it because they don't have the emotional capacity or brain development to process it. To dissociate means "to separate from." The trauma or memory is stored separately, "walled off" in the brain, mind, heart, and soul, allowing the person to go on with life. Some people describe going somewhere else during abuse, such as to a make-believe world. After abuse or trauma, the child often does not remember what happened unless something triggers that memory later in life.

A Broken Spirit

The Hebrew word for 'spirit' means wind, force, or energy. It refers to something being set in motion. The Old Testament uses this word to refer to God. Proverbs uses the word 21 times in different ways. In Proverbs 18:14, we get a good glimpse at the meaning of "spirit." The word describes a person's emotional energy and passion for life—the thing that moves them to take on the challenges of life.

'Spirit' in Proverbs articulates the psychological picture of the substance and mood of a person. The human spirit speaks to what goes on inside us in a deeply complex, nuanced, and multifaceted way. This complexity greatly overpowers the culture's attempts to explain such human spirit dynamics. Man's wisdom (sociology, philosophy, psychology) on these complex matters is incredibly reductionistic and struggles to see the varying facets and nuances of how God made the heart and spirit of people.

So, the crushed spirit in Proverbs 18 refers to the spirit that is losing or has lost the passion, desire, and energy to press into and deal with life. The crushed spirit has become broken, in large part due to the never-ending pursuit of the "one thing" in life that can bring happiness and hope. This spirit is not planted in the fear of the Lord and, therefore, is always at the mercy of the circumstances of life.

A Broken Heart

A brokenhearted person can literally feel the pain of brokenness. We have physiological responses to loss, grief, and hurtful situations. Emotional pain can be felt in a very real way in the body, the mind, and the heart. Our bodies are wired in such a way that emotional pain affects us physically. This is one reason it's so vital to get honest with our emotions and pursue healing— it impacts all of who we are and how we live.

Brokenheartedness can feel so intense because we do not have what we once did or what we thought we should have. We have lost something or someone. Also, we may feel all alone. Our body reacts to grief, anger, sadness, and fear. When we are in this place, our need for something beyond ourselves becomes more evident.

Our enemy would love to keep us from knowing God's love deeply and receiving the courage we need to move forward when life is hard. God loves to help us know Him and His presence with us, especially when life is hard.

Psalm 34:18 reminds us that God is not only present with us but near. Near to the pain we feel. Near to the loss we can't fill. Near to the needs we have and can't yet express.

- *For the brokenhearted, God gives nearness.* God is not removed from knowing about the pain or from our experience of pain. He is always available and close to those who suffer. Not only is He near, but He stays with us and will help us get through. He is not surprised or deterred, no matter how deep the brokenness feels.

- *God gives us the courage we need to breathe again.* Emotional pain sometimes leaves us speechless. This Psalm provides words to remind our hearts and talk to God when we cannot find the words ourselves. God's presence with us in our messy moments is of great comfort.

INTERACTIVE ACTIVITY (PART 1)

Embracing the Process of Breaking for Transformation

1. Reflect on a moment when you felt bound to break and what that breaking revealed about yourself and your purpose. Write a paragraph about your experience.

_____

_____

_____

_____

_____

_____

_____

_____

_____

_____

_____

2. Choose one of the Biblical accounts of breaking and anointing mentioned in the text (e.g. the woman anointing Jesus in Bethany) and summarize the symbolism and significance of the breaking process in that story.

_____

_____

_____

_____

_____

_____

_____

_____

_____

_____

_____

3. Applying the "Bound to Break" Concept: Explore the different definitions of "bound" provided in the text and identify how each definition relates to being bound to break in life situations. Write a short explanation for each definition.

_____
_____
_____
_____
_____
_____
_____
_____
_____
_____
_____

4. Breaking Free from Limitations: Discuss the different ways in which individuals can break free from limitations, whether through bondage, predestination, obligation, or connection. Provide examples of how one can actively embrace the breaking process for empowerment and growth.

_____
_____
_____
_____
_____
_____
_____
_____
_____
_____
_____

5. Personal Reflection: Reflect on your willingness to embrace the breaking process in your own life. Write about the challenges and rewards of breaking free from old patterns and limitations, and how you can move toward alignment with God's will and purpose through the breaking process.

_____

_____

_____

_____

_____

_____

_____

_____

_____

_____

_____

6. Application and Action: Develop a plan for embracing the process of breaking for transformation in your own life. Consider incorporating elements such as prayer, fasting, personal study, seeking wise counsel, and strengthening your faith. Reflect on the importance of finding a supportive community to help you through the breaking process.

_____

_____

_____

_____

_____

_____

_____

_____

_____

_____

_____

_____

7. Summarize the importance of breaking open for true freedom and purpose in God's plan for your life. Reflect on the concept that we are bound to break, and consider how embracing the process of transformation can lead to healing, deliverance, and alignment with God's divine purpose.

Remember, the breaking process may be challenging, but it is essential for growth and transformation in your journey toward wholeness and fulfilling your true potential.

INTERACTIVE ACTIVITY (PART 2)

1. What is the biblical definition of capacity?

    a) The ability to do something
    b) The maximum amount that something can hold
    c) The extent to which something can be filled

2. Which biblical character demonstrated great capacity when he built the ark?

    a) Noah
    b) Abraham
    c) Moses

3. According to the Bible, what should be our capacity for love?

    a) To love only those who love us
    b) To love our enemies
    c) To love our friends and family

4. In the biblical story of the loaves and fishes, what does this teach us about capacity?

    a) That our resources can be multiplied if we have faith
    b) To always give away what we have, no matter the amount
    c) That we should only share with those who are deserving

5. What does the Bible say about the capacity for forgiveness?

    a) To forgive only if the person apologizes
    b) To forgive without any conditions
    c) To forgive only if we forget the offense

6. Which biblical figure showed great capacity for patience?

    a) David
    b) Job
    c) Solomon

7. According to biblical teachings, what is the capacity of our physical bodies?

    a) Our bodies are limited and frail
    b) Our bodies are strong and invincible
    c) Our bodies have infinite potential

8. In the parable of the talents, what does this teach us about capacity?

    a) We should hide our talents and not share them with others
    b) We should use our talents for our own benefit
    c) We should use our talents to serve and multiply them

9. Which biblical character demonstrated great capacity for faith?

    a) Jonah
    b) Peter
    c) Thomas

10. According to the Bible, what is the capacity of God's love?

    a) Limited and conditional
    b) Unlimited and unconditional
    c) Varies depending on our behavior

11. How can one develop their capacity to its maximum potential according to the Bible?

a) By continuously seeking knowledge and learning new skills
b) By surrounding themselves with supportive and encouraging individuals
c) By setting goals and consistently working towards them
d) Through prayer, fasting, and living a consecrated life
e) All of the above

4. WHEN I BROKE, I HEALED
DON'T DELIVER HALF BAKED

God is building what's broken. He cannot build what's not broken. First you were broken and then you were healed! God's Word makes it clear that He restores those who are broken before Him. Oftentimes, He blesses you above measure—double for your trouble!

> *"Return to your stronghold, O prisoners of hope; today I declare that I will restore to you double."*
>
> — ZECHARIAH 9:12

> *"Instead of your shame, there shall be a double portion; instead of dishonor, they shall rejoice in their lot; therefore in their land, they shall possess a double portion; they shall have everlasting joy."*
>
> — ISAIAH 61:7

You may be wondering: What happened to cause the breaking in the natural sense? How is God going to use this for His glory? If I'm being real about the statement you're about to read, we often approach situations as if we're the victim. But I want to speak to those who are reading this book and have caused pain to someone else. It doesn't matter how others may view you; if you have a repentant heart, God will remove the shame and guilt from you because of the pain you caused. He will cast your sins into the sea of forgetfulness and cause them not to be remembered again. You can no longer walk around with the weight you're carrying.

"You will cast all our sins into the depths of the sea."

— MICAH 7:19

THE POWER OF FORGIVENESS

I saved you from yourself. I saved you from further damage that would have caused harm to you and everyone connected to you. I saved you from continuously carrying the hurt of the past, not knowing it was still a part of you. It was your past, but it did not pass; it is still in your heart, mind, soul, and spirit. You are carrying trauma like a trinket. It's almost like you can't live without it, but you can't live with it either. Trauma has brought many things that you continue to feed and nurture, which need to die.

Shame spoke for you when it was time for you to speak up and testify about what God did for you when He delivered you from addiction. Guilt spoke for you when you felt the need to lie to cover up your wrongs. Unforgiveness spoke for you because you believed forgiving meant letting someone off without consequences. Rejection spoke for you when you let others dictate who you would be to them without setting boundaries. Abandonment spoke for you when you stayed in toxic relationships, knowing it would lead to tragedy. Self-sabotage spoke for you when you chose self-pity instead of allowing God and those around you to help you break free. These are just a few examples.

There are so many people in the world whose broken stages in life look different. Some of you may have been broken by disappointment, starting in childhood when those who were supposed to protect you abandoned you. Others were betrayed by close friends who you thought were loyal. Some of you went through divorce—the separation of a connection you thought would last forever. You held your head down in shame, thinking, "How did this happen? The one God promised is now the one I'm walking away from. How can this be?" Maybe you desire a family, but your biological clock is ticking, or you feel unable to embrace having children again or ever. What do you do when your desires seem out of reach?

I'm reminded of the story of Hannah. She had a husband but deeply desired a child. It hurt her so much that it seemed nothing in life was more important than this child. She made a covenant with God, promising that if He allowed her to have a child, she would dedicate him to the Lord. I want to encourage anyone reading this book that it doesn't matter what you have lost or what you have not received yet. Rededicate your desires to God; lay them on the altar. If it is in God's plan, it will happen, but something in you must come into alignment with His will. When Hannah's perspective changed and she dedicated her son to God before even having him, Heaven responded. God doesn't want anything or anyone taking His place as number one in your life.

Recompense is coming; God will vindicate you. I recall the story of Joseph and how he was wrongly accused of trying to sleep with Pharaoh's wife and was put in prison. The Bible says that before long, the warden put Joseph in charge of all the other prisoners and everything that happened in the prison (Genesis 39:22). Even in prison, despite being wrongfully accused, God's favor on Joseph's life could not be stopped. We must remember who is in charge. You may have created your own personal prisons, but God says it's time to break out! You are owning the wrong place—it's time to take authority, exercise your gifts, and break free. God's grace and mercy will follow you. Walk through the door of your next building; they are following you. Walk through that bank and finance your business; they are following you. They are backing you up and will work on your behalf.

God once told me to speak whatever I needed because the angels are ready to work on my behalf. I want to encourage all of you who are disappointed because of closed doors. It's going to come in a way you least expect it. It won't come through who or how you think it should.

God will get the glory out of this one! This is for the books, and it's something only He can do! Get ready for God to do the miraculous, but the prerequisite is preparation. Are you prepared for the open door? Has your own agenda died completely so that when God begins to use you as He desires, your agenda won't get in the way? Offense will happen, but how will you respond? When hurt or talked about, will you choose to love and pray or gossip and complain? God is looking at our response before promotion. How much you have matured in life across the board will determine your next place. God has been showing us things, but now we must seek Him for revelation.

THE FOCAL POINT OF BUILDING

How can you build two entities at the same time? The process of creation often involves deconstruction to make way for something new. I have to break down what's built up to build it all over again. Taking what has been made and adorning it, molding, cutting, carving, and pruning until it's ready for its grand launch. How do we experience this process? This is through an open Heaven.

> *"Lord, open up your heavens and come down. Touch the mountains, and they will pour out smoke."*
>
> — PSALM 144:5-15

We can petition God to open the heavens. When the heavens open up to you, there is a transfer— there is total submission to His will.

> *"After Jesus was baptized, the heavens opened, and he saw the Spirit of God descend upon him."*
>
> — MATTHEW 3:16-17

After dying to yourself, you can ascend to your heavenly place.

"Therefore we are buried with Him by baptism into death, that just as Christ was raised up from the dead by the glory of the Father, even so we also should walk in newness of life."

— ROMANS 6:4

God is not just the one who helps you get through the day or personal trials. He is the one who empowers you to represent Him on earth. It's easy to get caught up in seeking relief from pain, forgetting that the purpose of pain is to produce growth and strength. We survived the pain to thrive in the next season of our lives. Pain is necessary for growth. You won't know how to survive until you're in an environment where you must. And once you've weathered the storm, you will thrive. Stagnation is like cement laid before the foundation, hindering movement and development. The finality of your situation will have you in a state of underdevelopment. It's time to break down, rebuild, and reach your full potential as a reflection of God's grace and power.

Whenever trauma would come into my life, I would talk to myself and say, "Crystal, hold it together. You have work to do. You don't have time to stop and address this. This is a distraction—no weapon formed against you shall prosper" (Isaiah 54:7). And I continued to declare the scripture until I felt the endurance to continue. The word of God is living, active, and sharper than any two-edged sword. So yes, use the word to combat the thoughts and attacks that come your way. God will fight for us if we hold our peace (Exodus 14:14). While this strategy of warfare is important, it doesn't negate that there is a wound. You are a wounded soldier and need healing. Imagine being injured physically, wiping off the blood, changing the battle clothes, and continuing on your journey without seeing a physician. The loss of blood will become fatal from losing too much. You then leave a trail of blood wherever you go. The weakness eventually appears evident because you are losing life by the minute, and you become infected. At this point, when you get to the hospital, your case has worsened because you failed to stop and accept that you were wounded.

Did you have on the armor that was needed for battle? Some of us do, and some don't. Does armor protect you from every attack?

According to the word of God, it's a good line of defense, but more is required to ensure the attacks don't penetrate. Penetrate what? Our minds, hearts, spirits, bodies, and souls. Though the outer exterior is protected, the interior is not fortified to withstand what's happening without and within.

Whatever was used to protect you in your own sense of understanding, God said, "I'm tearing it down. You are the altar. You will be the prophet. Be open to the spirit of prophecy coming over you and saying, 'God, what are you saying about my future that I'm missing?' I'm seeing cycles, God, break them." God said, "I want you to want Me."

Exodus 14:14 says, "The LORD will fight for you, and you shall hold your peace." This desire comes with consistent communication. Prayer is our mirror. The devil is trying to hinder our prayer life because prayer is how we see ourselves, how God sees us, and how His will is revealed. It is how we see the traps of the enemy, how the scales are removed from our eyes, how we hear more, and how chains are broken off us.

God's presence is like a time capsule where God takes us back and shows snapshots of the plan He already set in place. He then brings us back to reality and guides us on how to bring it to our present and future. If everyone worked in their gifts, imagine how it could all come together. God doesn't reveal everything to one person; He reveals it to all His children, and we help each other piece it together. We all come together as one, united instead of isolated, and each person plays a role in counteracting the enemy's attacks and whispers.

God is breaking down the false version of us that goes against His plan. Anything that stands in the way of God's will is evil and must be removed. Embracing who we truly are and walking in our identity is a process of stripping down the old, false self and allowing God to work through us.

The oil has changed. The garment you wore years ago is no longer needed in this season; it cannot be used because it's old. A computer software is updated just as a phone is updated. If you do not update your software on these devices, they will not operate correctly because Intel has shifted to a new way of operating—a new operating system. I often hear that when companies want to try a new operating system, they have to train all the employees to use it. It doesn't matter how long they have been with the company; everyone, whether they have tenure or not, has to be trained. So whether we have been saved for five, ten, or twenty years, or just five minutes, when God is doing something new, we have to humble ourselves and be ready for the shift. At any moment, He can give you something this week and something different next week, and it may sound totally different but will carry the same message. He's just expanding it. Are we really ready for true obedience—complete obedience to everything He says, even if it doesn't make sense to us at the moment?

WILL INSECURITIES CONTROL YOUR LIFE?

Don't let your insecurities drive you. Do you own your insecurities? Have you made them a part of who you are? Do insecurities shape your future?

I've been so accustomed to doing everything in a broken state—ministering to others, making power moves, hosting prayer gatherings, and counseling those in need of healing—but was I healed and whole? The brokenness in me is what caused me to break all the way open. We cannot allow what has happened and is happening to us to hold us back from breaking out of what has exiled us. We have the goodness of God locked up inside of us, and no one can benefit from the inheritance of God if we haven't died to ourselves.

> *"I affirm, brethren, by the boasting in you which I have in Christ Jesus our Lord, I die daily."*
>
> — 1 CORINTHIANS 15:31

> *"I am the resurrection and the life. He who believes in Me, though he may die, he shall live."*
>
> — JOHN 11:25

The old us is being buried every day. There are parts of us that are just scaling off, as we get closer to the Lord. The closer we get to what God promised, the more the old must be scaled off. Just like Jesus with Judas, He was betrayed but did nothing to him. His betrayal led to His death.

> "Then Judas, who had betrayed Him, when he saw that He was condemned, repented himself, and brought again the thirty pieces of silver to the chief priests and elders."
>
> — MATTHEW 27:3-10

When we begin to look at the things that have caused us pain in our lives, we will see that the pain killed something in us.

> "I consider that our present sufferings are not worth comparing with the glory that will be revealed in us."
>
> — ROMANS 8:18

The pain highlighted the issues, pointed me to the problem, and made me understand that I not only have to put my trust solely in God but also have the grace to forgive and learn how to let go to see the purpose of it all. Many of us have different forms of suffering, but embrace it for the breaking in you. Some may be saying: "The divorce broke me," "The lies broke me," "Facing my ugliness broke me," or "Tearing the walls down broke me." I want you to declare today, "I'm broken to be healed; I'm broken to be whole. What broke me processed me." I'm taking the scab off of you. The wound has healed, but the peeling of the scab is the wholeness.

ADJUSTMENT IN THE BROKEN PLACE

Imagine life as usual—you have made plans for the future. Whether single, divorced, with or without children, whether middle class or upper class, whether in ministry or just a churchgoer. Then something comes into your life that changes everything, causing you to question.

What was all that planning for when it comes to this ending? Why did I invest my time in the marriage if divorce was the finality? Why did I start the business if failure was going to be the byproduct? Was it a waste of time? Why buy a new car only for the company to recall it within a year? Why start the ministry when the support I had bailed on me? We have many questions, sometimes without immediate answers, and may never fully understand, but we still have to adjust.

What does 'adjust' mean according to the Oxford Dictionary? One definition is to alter or move something slightly in order to achieve the desired fit, appearance, or result. But another definition is to assess loss or damages when settling a claim.

I believe most of us can adjust to slight changes to fit where we're going in life and make room for the capacity of what we're receiving. But what happens when a dispute comes into play—especially a dispute that could potentially cause a detriment to your life, all that you have, and your future? At the point of adjustment, you assess the damage done and the loss that has taken place in your current situation.

"For I reckon that the sufferings of this present time are not worthy to be compared with the glory which shall be revealed in us."

— ROMANS 8:18

The true assessment is suffering for the sake of Christ. Loss in Christ is gain.

"For to me, to live is Christ and to die is gain."

— PHILIPPIANS 1:21

"It is a faithful saying: For if we be dead with him, we shall also live with him: If we suffer, we shall also reign with him: To reign with God."

— 2 TIMOTHY 2:11-13

DON'T DELIVER HALF-BAKED

Why is dysfunction sometimes considered normal? Dysfunctionalism is a state of underdevelopment, carried on by the normalization of disillusionment. The lack of development or growth is a result of the widespread acceptance of disappointment. Dysfunctionalism is when things are not working well or are not developing as they should. When people become used to feeling unhappy, disappointed, or unfulfilled, they stop trying to make things better or improve themselves and instead accept that things are just the way they are. This leads to underdevelopment and stagnation, where growth and improvement stop happening, and it becomes the norm. People who operate and function in a dysfunctional manner often don't realize it or aren't even aware that they are doing so.

COMFORTABILITY IN NORMALITY

This is why comfortability is a factor in the behavior of people who are accustomed to a way of living that God did not intend for them. They continue to go around the same circle, seeing the same thing, depending on the same measure of what God has done for years, and being satisfied with that when in fact, God truly has more that He wants to do if they are able to receive it. Dysfunctionalism plus disillusionment equals underdevelopment. This is why we have a world that is going round and round on the earth's axis and not reaching its full potential, because the world has not prayed for a revelation of how its function is supposed to be. Most of the people physically in power in the world are not godly men and women. This is why God has a kingdom government that will overthrow the human government and overpower those things that have been put in place to run the world in dysfunction. People continue to call evil good, and good evil.

> "Woe unto them that call evil good, and good evil; that put darkness for light, and light for darkness; that put bitter for sweet, and sweet for bitter!"

> — ISAIAH 5:20

BEFORE AND AFTER DEVASTATION COMES REVELATION

You receive a revelation of what's going to happen before it happens, during the process, and after. When it's meant for you to go through it, you will receive a revelation that gives you the fortitude to endure it and not rebuke it. That way, God can get the good out of you through it, and you won't miss the development of the purpose of it. God will not allow things to happen in our lives without a purpose behind them, using them for His glory, especially in His divine will for our lives. God releases blessings on the just as well as the unjust. He releases grace upon those whom He desires. But He also promises to preserve the Saints.

"God makes His sun rise on the evil and on the good, and sends rain on the just and on the unjust."

— MATTHEW 5:45

"I will have mercy on whom I will have mercy."

— ROMANS 9:15

"So it does not depend on the man who wills or on the man who runs, but on God who has mercy."

— ROMANS 9:16

"Love the LORD, all His faithful people! The LORD preserves those who are true to Him, but the proud He pays back in full."

— PSALM 31:23

BROKEN AGAIN TO BE RESET

After a bone is broken (fractured), the body will start the healing process. If the two ends of the broken bone are not lined up properly, the bone can heal with a deformity called a malunion. A malunion fracture occurs when a large space between the displaced ends of the bone has been filled in by new bone. Some people don't know what it feels like to operate from a healed place in any capacity of their lives. You can be so accustomed to dysfunction that dysfunction looks normal. Dysfunction becomes a way of life, and you don't even know that anything is wrong with the way you've been doing things because that's how you were formed. That's your natural way of being until you are shown something else and something is revealed to you. That is your normalcy.

Some of us have been so accustomed to operating in dysfunction that we can't even rejoice. My life, for a long period of time, was lived in depression, and I did not realize it until I was set free. I could not fully enjoy the joyous and victorious moments because there was always a dark cast over them. After I was set free from depression, I began to see that we can still function and move forward in life and not fully enjoy it, and have the joy of the Lord, which the Bible says is our strength. The joy of the Lord keeps strengthening us to go forward.

I understood why there was always a seesaw in my progression—because depression always had a foothold, along with everything else that comes with depression: anxiety, rejection, and abandonment. All of that led to the depression. It came in a cluster. So when I previously said, "This time you're going to do it whole," I understood it firsthand.

I have been doing ministry for years—bound, depressed, and broken. I still made progress, but within myself, I was not totally free and delivered. So, just imagine the effects we will have when we do it while being free. Also, remember that you didn't go through all that you went through for nothing. I didn't go through that process for nothing. I lived in self-pity. People were trying to help me get out of that state, and I kept making excuses as to why— almost like I deserved to be there, like this was going to be a part of my life. But the devil is a liar. That was not God's will. We may complain and say, "God, get me out," but God is saying, "Let me get it out of you so that you can be free." Stay in the fire and let God burn because God is a consuming fire. Let Him burn it up.

"We also glory in our sufferings, because we know that suffering produces perseverance; perseverance, character; and character, hope."

— ROMANS 5:3-4

THE BLESSING OF TRANSITION

Don't be hindered by your current place. You may have reservations about moving forward, but you are fighting the new you.

Many people are operating from a broken state, and those connected to them are getting the broken version of them—not the brokenness before God, but the broken, damaged part. You have not walked all the way through your healing, but you are trying to help others complete their process.

BROKEN BEFORE GOD & BROKEN FROM TRAUMA

Being broken before God will bring healing to the trauma. You can be broken before God and healed.

"For you will not delight in sacrifice, or I would give it; you will not be pleased with a burnt offering. The sacrifices of God are a broken spirit; a broken and contrite heart, O God, you will not despise."

— PSALM 51:16-17

DON'T SUFFOCATE YOUR PURPOSE

Don't suffocate your purpose with doubt, insecurity, and confusion. You have to break open so that you can live. Your purpose is locked up in a room with no oxygen, and Genesis teaches us that when God breathed into man, he became a living soul. Why is it that you won't let the breath of God breathe on your life so that you can live? So that your purpose can live, and so that your family can live? You have been locked up long enough; it's time to receive the wind of God.

You've been giving the world the crippled version of yourself, the broken version that says, "I don't want to do what I'm doing." Whatever God's purpose is for you, He will make you passionate about it. He will give you joy about it. You won't do it with the attitude of "I'm doing this because God said so," with a heart of reluctance. God will give you a love for what His purpose is for you, and you will do it with joy—not out of obligation, but out of passion to fulfill His purpose for your life.

ADDRESSING THE WOUND AND EMBRACING CHANGE

Listen, I want to speak to the wounded soldiers. Many of us have been wounded at some point in our lives, but somewhere along the way, we forgot to address the wound. I want you to declare: "It's time for me to address the wound." You may be wondering why everything seems so intense in your life right now. God is highlighting the wound, and pointing out the infected wounds that you forgot all about.

You may not feel the pain all the time, but every now and then, it shows up. But God is saying it's time to address the wound. He is the doctor who is fully equipped to heal you and equip you to keep going. We can't keep living and tolerating pain without addressing the root issue. God wants to show us that He is fully equipped to heal us and give us new life. We can no longer be hidden and tucked away. God has placed a life-changing purpose inside of you.

Jeremiah 29:11 reminds us that before we were formed in our mother's womb, God knew us, ordained us, appointed us, and anointed us. Yes, we may be dealing with issues right now, but that doesn't negate what God has placed inside of us. Declare this with me: "I am what change looks like." Allow God to come into your mind, heart, and life— give yourself totally to Him. God wants to heal you everywhere you hurt. He will take the pain away. Life won't be absent of pain, but God knew that this was the effect of sin. That's why He sent His Son Jesus to die ahead of time— *before* the pain, *before* the disappointment, and *before* the betrayal.

"O Death, where is your sting? O Hades, where is your victory?" The sting

of death is sin, and the strength of sin is the law. But thanks be to God, who gives us the victory through our Lord Jesus Christ."

— 1 CORINTHIANS 15:55-58

So yes, there may be pain ahead of time, but it was good that I was afflicted according to Psalm 119:71.

"It is good for me that I have been afflicted; that I might learn thy statutes."

— PSALM 119:71

Life gets stirred up sometimes because we need to know who God is and what He can do. So, just know that God is a healer, a counselor, and a restorer. He wants to show us that He is greater than what we're facing and that He will make a way of escape for us. It's time to address the wound and embrace change. Declare this with me: "I am what change looks like."

UPGRADE TIME

It's time to tell your baggage that you're making room for expansion. No longer will you tolerate things that you're no longer benefiting from. It's time to let go of the old and make room for the new. "It's time for my upgrade." Just like your phone needs an upgrade to function better, it's time for us to tap into God for our upgrade. He's getting ready to release an upgrade of power, authority, patience, love, integrity, righteousness, servanthood, and so much more. You have outgrown the place you're in. To receive this upgrade, you need to tap into a deeper intimacy with the Father. This requires more time, but it's necessary to receive the upgrade. It's time to elevate your prayer and study game. God is calling us out of the season of stagnation and into a season of progression and movement. "It's time to turn the page."

For some of you, the months to come may be difficult, but God is instructing you to move in another direction. As you turn the pages of your book, you'll begin to see that everything that was on the previous pages is not on the new ones. The script is changing for you, and you can't keep replaying the old episodes of your life. God is moving, so move with Him. You'll see why you had to shift. The path is different, but the story plot ends the same— God being glorified and you being in His divine will.

Don't be afraid to take a step into the unknown. It's time for an upgrade, and God is waiting for you to receive it. Upgrade time is here. It's time to let go of the old and make room for the new. God is calling you out of stagnation and into a season of progression and movement. It's time to elevate your prayer and study game, and it's time to move with God. Don't be afraid to take a step into the unknown. It's time for an upgrade, and God is waiting for you to receive it.

Don't Let Fear Paralyze You

Fear can be a paralyzing force in our lives, causing us to lose the ability to move forward, feel emotions, and be connect with others. Physically, we may experience a lack of energy; emotionally, we may become disconnected from others; spiritually, we may struggle to feel God's presence; and socially, we may avoid relationships altogether. But God is calling us to break free from this paralysis. God wants us to feel so that we can heal. We are reminded that the sufferings of the present are not worthy to be compared to the glory that shall be revealed in us. When we numb our pain with drugs, run from people or places, or avoid God's presence, we can cause damage that we may not even realize. But God is saying, "I want you to feel so that you can heal."

So how do we overcome fear? With faith. Faith comes by hearing the word of God. When we have fear, we are lacking faith. But when we trust in God's word, we can overcome fear.

> *"When I am afraid, I put my trust in you. In God, whose word I praise— in God I trust. I will not be afraid. What can man do to me?"*
>
> — PSALM 56:3-4

Speak over yourself and say: "I'm facing my giant head-on, and I'm moving forward." It's not a matter of if He is or even when—I just need to know that He is. Fear can hold us back from experiencing all that God has for us. But God is calling us to break free from this paralysis and live a life of faith and trust. Remember that faith comes by hearing the word of God, and when we trust in His word, we can overcome fear. Don't let fear hold you back any longer. Declare, "I'm facing my giant head-on, and I'm moving forward." It's time to take control of your life and move forward with faith.

INTERACTIVE ACTIVITY

Fill in the blanks based on what we've discussed so far. The answer key is located in the back of the book.

1. Building What's Broken: God can't build what's not _____ . The process of creation often involves deconstruction to make way for something _____ ." I have to break down what's built up to build it all over again."

2. Open Heaven: Pain is necessary for growth, but shouldn't just be a means of seeking _____ . The purpose of pain is to produce _____ and strength, not just temporary relief from personal trials.

3. Surviving to Thrive: _____ hinders movement and development, leading to _____ . Embracing the journey of breaking down, rebuilding, and reaching one's full potential is essential in reflecting God's _____ and power.

4. Armor for Battle: While the armor protects the outer exterior, the interior needs _____ to withstand attacks on the mind, heart, spirit, body, and soul. Complete obedience to God's guidance, even when it doesn't make _____ , is vital for true growth and development.

5. Learning from Dysfunction: Some people are so accustomed to dysfunction that it becomes _____ , hindering their ability to operate from a healed place in any aspect of life. Operating in brokenness before God can lead to _____ from trauma and a genuine transformation.

6. Psalm 51: 16-17 declares, "For you will not delight in sacrifice, or I would give it; you will not be pleased with a burnt offering. The sacrifices of God are a _____ spirit; a _____ and contrite heart, O God, you will not despise."

7. Romans 5: 3-4 declares: "We also glory in our sufferings, because we know that suffering _____ perseverance; perseverance, _____ ; and _____ , hope."

8. The Blessing of Transition: Don't be hindered by your current place that you have _____ about moving forward. You are fighting the _____ you.

9. Broken Before God: Being broken before God will bring healing to the _____ .

10. You can be broken before God and _____ .

5. Broken to Build
I'm Building Something

How would you know what needs to be fixed if you don't take it apart? The object at hand isn't working properly, so there has to be a repair. Sometimes, whether it's our cars or different manufacturing machines, we can detect that something is wrong, but we won't know what it is unless we go inside the system and investigate. If the issue isn't immediately noticeable, we have to remove the outer layer to see where the problem lies. As you dig deeper, you might discover other issues leading up to the main one. At this point, you have two options to address the situation.

As you investigate the main issue, you can either stop and address each problem one at a time, or you can break the whole thing down and rebuild it from scratch. I've encountered situations where people would suggest, "Let's just patch it up." It's going to cost too much to fix the whole thing right now, and that's money you don't have, so a patch job seems like the only option until you can afford a new part. In this scenario, you might even opt for a used part to replace the damaged one because, while it's not new, it's still functional enough to get some more wear and tear out of it before it, too, is considered damaged.

In other words, you're trying to buy some time—whether it's to gather up funds or to muster the nerve to embrace something entirely new. When we consider the time, money, energy, and stress involved in not demolishing the whole thing, especially when a patch job just won't suffice, we might find ourselves living in regret because we moved forward without fully addressing the matter. Sometimes, we focus so much on the aesthetics of how things appear that we overlook the core of the issue, which might have eaten away at us so severely that we wonder if recovery is even possible.

As the rain pours down in your life, as the broken pieces scatter, you decide, for once in your life, to be broken. For once, you decide to do things differently. For once, you take that leap of faith and trust God to demolish one thing so He can build something new in you.

"Behold, I will do a new thing; now it shall spring forth; shall ye not know it?"

— ISAIAH 43:19

God wants you to see the finished work. He wants you to understand that what you see right now is not the finality of your situation. Your Father wants you to grasp that this is the beginning of the new thing.

While you grieve or have grieved for what was and what could've been, God says, "Look forward and embrace what shall be in Heaven, and so shall it be here on earth." What you are feeling right now will be a distant memory—a testimony of what God can do.

"I will give you the keys of the kingdom of heaven; whatever you bind on earth will be bound in heaven, and whatever you loose on earth will be loosed in heaven."

— MATTHEW 16:19

Heaven has your answer, and Heaven will respond on your behalf, but you have to use your keys. Take a moment to think about keys. When you lock something, it means that there is something of value you don't want everyone to have access to. When someone has a key to anything I own, it means I trust them with what's behind the door. Not having a key is the only thing stopping us from walking through the door. There may be windows that could make what's protected accessible, but entry through those windows would be illegal because they are not meant to be walked through. So when the Lord says in His Word that we have keys, you better believe there is something that the key will unlock for you that everyone doesn't have access to. What will you do with that access? Will you value and cherish it, or will you abandon and mishandle it?

How Do You Access a Key?

A key is given upon revelation from God. Let's look at the previous scriptures in Matthew 16:

> *"When Jesus came to the region of Caesarea Philippi, he asked his disciples, 'Who do people say the Son of Man is?' They replied, 'Some say John the Baptist; others say Elijah; and still others, Jeremiah or one of the prophets.' 'But what about you?' he asked. 'Who do you say I am?'*
>
> — MATTHEW 16:13-15

Jesus asked all of His disciples, "Who do people say that I am?" They gave their responses of what others said He was. Then, He asked them specifically who He was.

The people abroad were not walking with Jesus every day; they could not have a one-on-one experience. And out of all of them, only one responded with the revelation of who Jesus is. Peter was one of the first disciples chosen to follow Jesus and the first to receive the revelation of who He is. He was also the first to preach after Jesus' ascension and the arrival of the Holy Spirit, and 3,000 souls gave their lives to Christ.

Let's read about what took place in Acts 2:14-42.

Acts 2:14-42

¹⁴ Then Peter stepped forward with the eleven other apostles and shouted to the crowd, "Listen carefully, all of you, fellow Jews and residents of Jerusalem! Make no mistake about this.

¹⁵ These people are not drunk, as some of you are assuming. Nine o'clock in the morning is much too early for that.

¹⁶ No, what you see was predicted long ago by the prophet Joel:"

¹⁷ "In the last days," God says, "I will pour out my Spirit upon all people. Your sons and daughters will prophesy. Your young men will see visions, and your old men will dream dreams.

¹⁸ In those days I will pour out my Spirit even on my servants— men and women alike— and they will prophesy.

¹⁹ And I will cause wonders in the heavens above and signs on the earth below— blood and fire and clouds of smoke.

²⁰ The sun will become dark, and the moon will turn blood red before that great and glorious day of the Lord arrives.

²¹ But everyone who calls on the name of the Lord will be saved."

²² People of Israel, listen! God publicly endorsed Jesus the Nazarene by doing powerful miracles, wonders, and signs through him, as you well know.

²³ But God knew what would happen, and His prearranged plan was carried out when Jesus was betrayed. With the help of lawless Gentiles, you nailed him to a cross and killed him.

²⁴ But God released him from the horrors of death and raised him back to life, for death could not keep him in its grip.

²⁵ King David said this about him: "I see that the Lord is always with me. I will not be shaken, for he is right beside me.

²⁶ No wonder my heart is glad, and my tongue shouts his praises! My body rests in hope.

²⁷ For you will not leave my soul among the dead or allow your Holy One to rot in the grave.

²⁸ You have shown me the way of life, and you will fill me with the joy of your presence."

²⁹ Dear brothers, think about this! You can be sure that the patriarch David wasn't referring to himself, for he died and was buried, and his tomb is still here among us.

³⁰ But he was a prophet, and he knew God had promised with an oath that one of David's own descendants would sit on his throne.

³¹ David was looking into the future and speaking of the Messiah's resurrection. He was saying that God would not leave him among the dead or allow his body to rot in the grave.

³² God raised Jesus from the dead, and we are all witnesses of this.

³³ Now He is exalted to the place of highest honor in heaven, at God's right hand. And the Father, as He had promised, gave Him the Holy Spirit to pour out upon us, just as you see and hear today.

³⁴ For David himself never ascended into heaven, yet he said,

'The Lord said to my Lord, 'Sit in the place of honor at my right hand

³⁵ until I humble your enemies, making them a footstool under your feet.''

³⁶ So let everyone in Israel know for certain that God has made this Jesus, whom you crucified, to be both Lord and Messiah!

³⁷ Peter's words pierced their hearts, and they said to him and to the other apostles, "Brothers, what should we do?"

³⁸ Peter replied, "Each of you must repent of your sins and turn to God, and be baptized in the name of Jesus Christ for the forgiveness of your sins. Then you will receive the gift of the Holy Spirit.

³⁹ This promise is to you, to your children, and to those far away —all who have been called by the Lord our God."

⁴⁰ Then Peter continued preaching for a long time, strongly urging all his listeners, "Save yourselves from this crooked generation!"

⁴¹ Those who believed what Peter said were baptized and added to the church that day—about 3,000 in all.

⁴² All the believers devoted themselves to the apostles' teaching, to fellowship, to sharing in meals (including the Lord's Supper), and to prayer.

As we continue examining Peter, let's focus on a scripture in Matthew that highlights his spiritual progression:

"Simon Peter answered, 'You are the Messiah, the Son of the living God.' Jesus replied, 'Blessed are you, Simon son of Jonah, for this was not

revealed to you by flesh and blood, but by my Father in heaven. And I tell
you that you are Peter, and on this rock I will build my church, and the
gates of Hades will not overcome it.'"

— Matthew 16:16-17

Look at the progression of how Peter is addressed. Matthew called
him Simon Peter, and then Jesus called him Simon, son of Jonah. He
blessed him, acknowledged his natural lineage, and then gave him a revelation that could only be articulated because of his readiness to receive.
Jesus then called Peter "the rock," meaning His church can only be built
on the revelation of who the Father is through Jesus Christ.

The name Peter is derived from the Hebrew name "Kepha" (כֵּפָה),
which means "rock" or "stone".) In Hebrew, the name "Jonah" (יוֹנָה) is
derived from the Hebrew word "yona" (יוֹנָה), which means "dove". The
name Jonah is often interpreted as "dove" or "pigeon" and is thought to
symbolize peace, innocence, and purity.

3 Progressions:

1. Simon
2. Peter, son of Jonah
3. Peter

Peter also denied Jesus three times.

"Then they seized Him and led Him away, bringing Him into the high
priest's house, and Peter was following at a distance. And when they had
kindled a fire in the middle of the courtyard and sat down together, Peter
sat down among them. Then a servant girl, seeing him as he sat in the
light and looking closely at him, said, "This man also was with
Him." But he denied it, saying, "Woman, I do not know Him." And a
little later, someone else saw him and said, "You also are one of them."
But Peter said, "Man, I am not." And after an interval of about an
hour, still another insisted, saying, "Certainly this man also was with
Him, for he too is a Galilean." But Peter said, "Man, I do not know what

you are talking about." And immediately, while he was still speaking, the rooster crowed. 61 And the Lord turned and looked at Peter. And Peter remembered the saying of the Lord, how He had said to him, "Before the rooster crows today, you will deny Me three times." And he went out and wept bitterly."

— LUKE 22:54-62

Within Peter's journey, there was also a death. Peter left his old life behind and followed Jesus.

"Jesus was walking by the Sea of Galilee. He saw two brothers. They were Simon (also called Peter) and Andrew, his brother. They were putting a net into the sea, for they were fishermen. Jesus said to them, "Follow Me, and I will make you fishers of men!" At once they left their nets and followed Him."

— MATTHEW 4:18-22

Everything portrayed was part of Peter's dying process to get to the rock; Jesus acclimates Peter.

"When they had finished eating, Jesus said to Simon Peter, 'Simon son of John, do you love Me more than these?' 'Yes, Lord,' he said, 'you know that I love You.' Jesus said, 'Feed My lambs.' Again Jesus said, 'Simon son of John, do you love Me?' He answered, 'Yes, Lord, you know that I love You.' Jesus said, 'Take care of My sheep.' The third time He said to him, 'Simon son of John, do you love Me?' Peter was hurt because Jesus asked him the third time, 'Do you love Me?' He said, 'Lord, You know all things; You know that I love You.' Jesus said, 'Feed My sheep. Very truly I tell you, when you were younger, you dressed yourself and went where you wanted; but when you are old, you will stretch out your hands, and someone else will dress you and lead you where you do not want to go.' Jesus said this to indicate the kind of death by which Peter would glorify God. Then He said to him, 'Follow Me!'"

— JOHN 21:15-19

Now, the new Peter is resurrected with revelation. To receive the key, a revelation of who God is releases to us who we are and gives us the authority to walk in power on the earth because we are seated in heavenly places.

"I have given you authority to trample on snakes and scorpions and to overcome all the power of the enemy; nothing will harm you."

— LUKE 10:19

"So even if I boast somewhat freely about the authority the Lord gave us for building you up rather than tearing you down, I will not be ashamed of it."

— 2 CORINTHIANS 10:18

"And hath raised us up together, and made us sit together in heavenly places in Christ Jesus."

— EPHESIANS 2:6

We are seated with Christ in heavenly places. Joint-seating with Christ is 'far above' all principalities and powers of darkness. God is changing my storyline, but it has to be revealed. We need the script to walk out the life that God has ordained for us.

In the New Testament, the two primary Greek words that describe Scripture are 'logos' and 'rhema.' Logos refers to the total inspired Word of God, often used to describe Jesus as the living Word, as found in John 1:1, Luke 8:11, and Hebrews 4:12. On the other hand, 'rhema' refers specifically to a spoken word or utterance, as used in Luke 1:38, 3:2, and Acts 11:16.

God is the breath of life, and He is the living Word that transforms us. When will we decide to build according to His divine word for our lives? Could it be that the results we are expecting are not happening as planned because somewhere along the way, we veered away from His plan? The storms of life come to detour us, and many times we don't even recognize that we have taken an alternative route outside the scope of God's plan. How do you determine which path is right?

"My sheep hear my voice, and I know them, and they follow me."

— JOHN 10:27

Sometimes we don't see and understand the accessibility we have to God, our Father in Heaven. Being a follower of Jesus Christ allows us to receive intel from Heaven.

"The steps of a good man are ordered by the Lord, And He delights in his way."

— PSALM 37:23

There has to be continuous communing with our Father.

"But you, when you pray, go into your room, and when you have shut your door, pray to your Father who is in the secret place; and your Father who sees in secret will reward you openly."

— MATTHEW 6:6-7

This isn't second-hand information about what is and what's to come. This is coming straight from our source of everything we need as it pertains to life. Don't be distracted by the storms that enter your life.

While you are driving in the storm, you can barely see the road ahead, but you have your headlights on, and the word of God says:

"Thy word is a lamp unto my feet, and a light unto my path."

— PSALM 119:105

"For in it the righteousness of God is revealed from faith to faith; as it is written, 'The just shall live by faith.'"

— Romans 1:17

Looking into the distance, it may seem blurry, it may not seem clear; you may wonder if you're going to reach your destination on time. You may not understand why things are happening the way they are. You may wonder if you still have purpose. You may wonder if all of what you did up until this point was even worth it. God even recognizes all that you contributed to your life with a heart to serve, with a heart that desires to please Him. I know you're wondering if He saw the tears, if He heard the prayers, if He remembers the sleepless nights when you cried out to Him for help. I'm here to tell you that your help is the change, your help is the sudden move, your help is the decision to follow after what God has for you to be and do in the earth. You cannot worry about anybody else's journey. The Bible says:

"Be anxious for nothing, but in everything by prayer and supplication with thanksgiving, let your requests be made known to God; and the peace of God, which surpasses all understanding, will guard your hearts and minds through Christ Jesus."

— Philippians 4:6-7

He said He will keep us in perfect peace if we keep our minds stayed on Him. Don't worry about what's broken because He's making all things new. He's using new raw materials to build this new thing.

"I'm breaking you down to build you back up again. I'm reestablishing your foundation so that when you begin to live your life, you will not live it the same way. I'm building you up in every area. I am testing you to see how you can handle the normalities of life—the daily disappointments that may come your way. How will you respond to life's challenges? How can I give you more to do and add more to your schedule and pour out a greater anointing

if you're not able to handle the things that happen in the course of life? I am putting on a different weight of responsibility in the spirit realm. I'm testing you with natural things to handle things in the spirit. I am teaching you how to use your spiritual weapons to navigate through life's issues and circumstances. Will you learn how to live in the spirit realm and not respond in your flesh, in your natural abilities, in your natural ways of responding? I'm showing you how to allow the Holy Spirit to be your first responder to every situation. I am opening your eyes to see clearly how to go through life My way."

How do you live life God's way?

It is in your time of daily communion and prayer with God, your Father, that you can position yourself to hear His voice.

"My sheep hear My voice, and I know them, and they follow Me: And I give unto them eternal life; and they shall never perish, neither shall any man pluck them out of My hand."

— JOHN 10:27-28

Position yourself to hear, and when you hear His voice, follow Him. What He will release to you will lead you into eternal life. His directions in the short-term, temporary situation will lead you into eternity in paradise with your Father. Nothing that you are trying to accomplish will perish because it is made in eternity, it is created and established in eternity. This means that it will last forever.

"Do not lay up for yourselves treasures on earth, where moth and rust destroy and where thieves break in and steal; but lay up for yourselves treasures in heaven, where neither moth nor rust destroys and where thieves do not break in and steal. For where your treasure is, there your heart will be also."

— MATTHEW 6:19-21

"God is faithful to His promises, and what He promises His people—
salvation, life, and inheritance—is eternal and incorruptible."

— HEBREWS 10:32-34

Everything that we establish here is wrapped up and consumed in
salvation— the salvation of our soul, body, and spirit.

*"For you know that God paid a ransom to save you from the empty life
you inherited from your ancestors. And it was not paid with mere gold or
silver, which lose their value. It was the precious blood of Christ, the sinless,
spotless Lamb of God."*

— 1 PETER 1:18-19

We were bought with a price; we have value. We cannot let anyone
devalue who we are in Christ.

*"You were bought with a price [you were actually purchased with the
precious blood of Jesus and made His own]. So then, honor and glorify
God with your body."*

— 1 CORINTHIANS 6:20

When we know who we belong to and the cross we carry, it won't be
easy for us to fall into the traps of the enemy. This is why every part of us
has to be submitted to the Lord. This is not an overnight process, but a
very intentional one that we have to undertake daily for the rest of our
lives. When we think about brokenness, we might automatically think
of heartbreak, and that's understandable because our heart is the center
of our being. It's where our passion lies. It's what drives us to do what
we do. This is also why God wants our whole heart.

*"That if you confess with your mouth the Lord Jesus and believe in your
heart that God has raised Him from the dead, you will be saved. For with*

the heart one believes unto righteousness, and with the mouth confession is
made unto salvation."

— ROMANS 10:9-10

Out of our mouths comes the confession that our hearts first believed. We pronounce this confession by faith. So, in your heart, you believe that you could be made righteous, and it is sealed when you confess it with your mouth, coming into agreement with what the scripture says. After you have believed and received, it is sealed until the day of redemption.

"And do not grieve the Holy Spirit of God, by whom you were sealed and
marked [branded as God's own] for the day of redemption [the final
deliverance from the consequences of sin]."

— EPHESIANS 4:30

God is dealing with the finality of things. The things of this earth are temporary; our time here is just a moment, as Job said.

"Yet you do not know [the least thing] about what may happen tomorrow.
What is the nature of your life? You are [really] but a wisp of vapor (a
puff of smoke, a mist) that is visible for a little while and then disappears
[into thin air]."

— JAMES 4:14

Yes, this is a metaphorical scripture, but if we look at other scriptures that connect to this, we can understand how God views time.

"But, beloved, do not be ignorant of this one thing, that one day is with the
Lord as a thousand years, and a thousand years as one day."

— 2 PETER 3:8

According to an article written by Matt King and Christopher Watson from the University of Tasmania, over the past few decades, Earth's rotation around its axis—which determines how long a day is—has been speeding up. This trend has been making our days shorter; in fact, in June 2022, we set a record for the shortest day over the past half a century or so.

BREAKTHROUGH — BREAKOUT — BREAK FORTH

What process are you in right now? As we close this book, I want to share with you what happens when it's time for a major catapult in your life. You have what we call a *Divine Disruption.* God says, "I'm disrupting your life to save your life."

The Merriam-Webster dictionary says that *disrupt* comes from the Latin *disrumpere*, which is formed by combining *dis-* ("apart") and *rumpere* ("to break").

God said, "I can't form what I can't break." This tells us that disruption isn't bad, especially when it's divine. In an article excerpt by Sarah Townsend, she says, "Disruption is not only the point where something is interrupted, or broken, or changed. It is also the point where something better is created, where something new improves what it breaks, and where the interruption is just the beginning point for what is to come."

Some of you who are reading this book, I want you to take a moment and stop and lift your hands and say, "Thank you, Jesus, for interrupting my plans." If our plans had turned out the way we wanted them to, we would never see what God originally designed for us to have in our lives. I want to talk to the person who is disappointed in what they believe God spoke to them, something they believe belonged to them. He may have said it five years ago, and it just didn't turn out the way you thought. Did God change His mind? Yes, He does.

One example of God changing His mind in the Bible is found in Exodus 32:14, when Moses interceded on behalf of the Israelites after they had sinned by worshiping the golden calf. The verse states, "So the Lord changed His mind about the harm which He said He would do to

His people." This illustrates how our prayers and actions can lead to a change in God's planned course of action.

> *"In my distress I called to the Lord; I cried to my God for help. From His temple He heard my voice; my cry came before Him, into His ears."*
>
> — PSALM 18:6

> *"Then you will call on me and come and pray to me, and I will listen to you."*
>
> — JEREMIAH 29:12

God will indeed listen and respond to our cry. God's plan is a collective effort. It takes more than one person to fulfill the vision of your life. God needs a yes and total surrender from you and not only you but all of the people that are connected to you. You're going to have those who help you build and those who will try to deter you from your vision. But we will have both in our lives to help us grow and get to where we need to be. Disruption challenges us to be more like Christ.

> *"If your enemy is hungry, feed him; if he is thirsty, give him something to drink. In doing this, you will heap burning coals on his head. Do not be overcome by evil, but overcome evil with good."*
>
> — ROMANS 12:20-21

This passage demonstrates the importance of responding to hostility with kindness, ultimately allowing us to break the cycle of animosity and promote peace.

> *"I saved you from yourself. I saved you from further damage you would have caused yourself and everyone connected to you in the new year. I saved you from continuously walking around with the hurt of the past, not realizing that it was still a part of you. It was your past, but it did not pass. It is still in your heart, mind, soul,*

and spirit. You are carrying around the trauma like a trinket. It's almost like you can't live without it, but you can't live with it. What I mean is that the trauma brought several things that you continue to feed and nurture, where these particular areas need to die."

- *Shame*: Your shame spoke for you when it was time to tell your testimony about how God delivered you from addiction.

- *Guilt*: Guilt spoke for you when you felt the need to cover up your wrongdoings or past hurts with lies.

- *Unforgiveness*: Unforgiveness spoke for you when you hesitated to forgive others, fearing they wouldn't pay for their actions.

- *Rejection*: Rejection spoke for you when you allowed people to define your worth without setting boundaries.

- *Abandonment*: Abandonment spoke for you when you remained in toxic relationships despite knowing they would lead to harm.

- *Self-sabotage*: Self-sabotage spoke for you when you chose self-pity over seeking help to break free.

These are just a few examples of how these negative emotions keep speaking for you, holding you back from living your best life.

So let's get back to the question at hand: Does God change His mind? 2 Corinthians 1:20 affirms the unwavering nature of God's promises by stating, "For no matter how many promises God has made, they are 'Yes' in Christ. And so through Him the 'Amen' is spoken by us to the glory of God." This verse emphasizes that all of God's promises are fulfilled and affirmed through Christ, and believers are called to respond with their own resounding affirmation ("Amen") to acknowledge and give glory to God's faithfulness in keeping His word.

After reading this passage and explanation, do we understand what is translated here? The promises are *yes —in Christ*! Can we forfeit a promise if we are not in Christ? The answer is yes. So the "Amen" is spoken by us to the glory of God, so we as believers have to come in agreement with the promise of God to the glory of God. How do our lives bring Him glory?

> *"And whatever you do, whether in word or deed, do it all in the name of the Lord Jesus, giving thanks to God the Father through Him."*
>
> — COLOSSIANS 3:17

We as believers are to approach every aspect of our lives with gratitude and a focus on honoring Jesus Christ through our actions and speech. By dedicating all that we do to the Lord and expressing thankfulness to God, we can embody His presence and bring glory to His name in all that we undertake. Our deeds that glorify God can bring us rewards in both this life and in eternity. But deeds that don't glorify Him can hold back what He promised to us.

In Matthew 6:19-20, Jesus instructs His followers to store up treasures in heaven by prioritizing spiritual investments over earthly gains. Hebrews 11:6 states that God is a rewarder of those who diligently seek Him, indicating that our faithful obedience and service to Him will not go unnoticed or unrewarded. Ultimately, while the rewards may vary, the satisfaction of living a life that honors God and aligns with His will is the greatest reward of all.

THE REWARD FOR THE UNBELIEVER

> *"All unrighteousness is sin. Therefore, anything contrary to righteousness is considered sinful in the eyes of God."*
>
> — 1 JOHN 5:17

"For the wages of sin is death, but the gift of God is eternal life in
Christ Jesus our Lord."

— ROMANS 6:23

Choosing to sin leads to spiritual death or premature physical death and
separation from God, while righteousness through Christ offers the gift
of eternal life.

Can deeds determine if we receive the promises of God? Yes or No?
So, yes, our deeds can sometimes determine if we receive some of God's
promises. We have to remember God's grace and sovereignty in
choosing whom to extend grace to in Romans 9:15-16, which says, "For
He says to Moses, 'I will have mercy on whom I have mercy, and I will
have compassion on whom I have compassion.' So then, it depends not
on human will or deeds, but on God who has mercy."

Conditional Promises

Conditional promises can be found in 1 John 1:9, which states, "If
we confess our sins, He is faithful and just to forgive us our sins and to
cleanse us from all unrighteousness." The condition of confession is a
prerequisite for receiving God's forgiveness and restoration.

James 4:8 says, "Draw near to God, and He will draw near to you."
Our proximity to God and the depth of our relationship with Him is
directly related to our willingness to seek Him and make the effort to
draw closer.

Unconditional Promises

*"For I know the plans I have for you, declares the Lord, plans for welfare
and not for evil, to give you a future and a hope."*

— JEREMIAH 29:11

"So do not fear, for I am with you; do not be dismayed, for I am your

God. I will strengthen you and help you; I will uphold you with my right-eous right hand."

— ISAIAH 41:10

THE BUILDING PROCESS

"Be patient because I'm building something," is a gentle reminder that resonates with the essence of prayer as portrayed in the Bible, where over 650 prayers are recorded, including 25 poignant prayers from Jesus Himself. The act of prayer transcends mere words—it is a transformative encounter where you touch God, and He, in turn, touches you, setting a profound trajectory with no return to the past.

In the pursuit of Glory, 2 Corinthians 3:18 illuminates our journey from one level of glory to another as we behold the reflection of the Lord's glory, undergoing a metamorphosis by the Spirit's guidance. Matthew 18:19-20 beckons believers to unite in prayer, invoking the promise that agreement in prayer unlocks divine intervention from the heavenly Father, setting the stage for a courtroom of heaven experience.

As we delve into the book of Revelation, penned by John the Beloved, we are reminded of his initial address to the seven churches of Asia, laying the foundation for prophetic revelations to unfold. This journey invites introspection, acknowledging the call and anointing on our lives, unveiling the mysteries of purpose amidst the ebb and flow of our spiritual paths. May this exploration ignite a fervor for prayer, leading us from glory to glory as we venture through the realms of divine encounters and heavenly decrees.

UNVEILING THE PLOT TWIST

This message echoes beyond just mothers; it encompasses all individuals carrying valuable treasures within them and willing to unleash them into the world—it's an urgent call to action. As we ponder our capacity for the next chapter, a divine interruption challenges us to realize that there is always more in the depths of God's presence, determined by our hunger for closeness with Him.

The story of John embarking on the journey of recording the book of Revelation brings us to a place where a heavenly door beckons for a deeper revelation. The call to ascend into the Spirit's realm unveils a transcendent perspective, urging us to see ourselves as God sees us, recognizing our true identity in Him. Through this revelation, the focus shifts from our outward actions to the transformation of our inner character and spiritual disciplines, emphasizing the pursuit of God's will over personal status or accomplishments.

In spite of the complexities of our stories lie unforeseen plot twists orchestrated by God, shaping our destinies in ways we never imagined. Some twists are the enemy's design, while others stem from our own choices, yet God's hand guides us through suspenseful moments, inviting us to trust His divine narrative. As disciples of God, our lives become testimonies of His glory through the acts we perform, reflecting His sanctity and establishing His Kingdom on earth. Join this expedition of faith as God unravels mysteries, reveals His plans, and empowers us to live out His divine purpose with unwavering dedication and unyielding grace.

Amidst the call to action, a profound message resonates—no more blending, no compromise. What occurs behind closed doors, whether good or bad, is under divine scrutiny, signaling a time of reckoning when secret seeds sown will bear fruit openly. Delving deeper, God seeks to heal and deliver, releasing individuals from personal struggles and fostering a sense of accountability in the body of Christ.

As stewards of God's Kingdom, unity becomes paramount, highlighting the interconnectedness of believers in upholding the effectiveness of the collective body. Fostering a culture of support rather than reproach, God orchestrates a holistic transformation—not merely mending fragmented pieces but propelling individuals towards expansion and alignment with His divine purpose. Through extraction, adjustment, and the shedding of performance-driven expectations, God rebuilds from within, leading His people from comfort to engagement and ministry to intimacy.

The journey from point A to point Z is not without effort, demanding a shift in focus from external validations to inner growth and from fragmented existence to divine alignment. God's call to reboot and realign challenges individuals to embrace transformation, willingly surrendering to His refining process for the sake of His Kingdom. As the plot twists in our lives unfold, may we heed the call to deeper intimacy, communal responsibility, and individual authenticity on the path to fulfilling God's greater purpose.

RISING FROM THE RUBBLE

In a journey marked by perseverance and commitment to seeing things through to completion, the importance of enduring transitions to reach a desired outcome is highlighted. Understanding that each step in the process is integral to development, the narrative underscores the power of words in shaping the life God intends for His people. Drawing inspiration from figures like Ezra, Zerubbabel, and Nehemiah, as well as Jesus' inner circle of Peter, James, and John, the narrative delves into the significance of surrounding oneself with individuals who can navigate the challenges of warfare and offer support in times of rebuilding.

The theme of rebuilding, echoed in the Babylonians' destruction of Jerusalem to prevent its easy reconstruction, speaks to the vulnerability and resilience of God's people in the face of adversity. As the narrative unfolds, the notion of building takes on both a physical and metaphorical significance, emphasizing the permanent establishment of God's work within individuals during pivotal seasons of transformation. Through the process of shaping and constructing, the body of Christ finds itself in a season of rebuilding, prompting introspection on the reasons for past brokenness to prevent recurrence in the future.

As God continues to lay the foundation for lasting restoration and transformation, individuals are challenged to reassess their inner circles, rebuild from the core, and confront vulnerabilities with faith and fortitude. With each chapter revealing layers of divine construction and personal growth, the narrative unfolds as a testament to the enduring power of faith and perseverance in the journey toward wholeness and divine purpose.

Divine Blueprints: Embracing God's Design for Renewal

Have you ever pondered the concept of modular homes—pre-built, furnished, and awaiting only the payment for land to complete their purpose? Much like these homes, God has already stored every aspect of your life in heaven, awaiting your call to bring them forth on earth. In the symbolic imagery of the four winds in 2024, representing the breath and presence of God, a journey unfolds, four years post-pandemic, where divine winds gather and spread abundance.

The wind of God is stirred by prophecy and action, initiating transformative movements post-pandemic and beyond. Each year since the crisis holds profound significance, from the unity and establishment of the triune God in 2021 to the spiritual division and union in 2022, paving the way for completion and resurrection in 2023, leading to the finality of creation on the fourth day in 2024.

As the Hebrew word for "seasons," or moed, denotes divine appointments in Genesis, God orchestrates a comprehensive strategy, covering all facets to expose and overcome the enemy. This year marks a season of restructuring, where the infrastructure of your life undergoes a divine renovation. You are called to allow God to gut out the old, tear down existing barriers, and make space for new developments, expanding the very foundation of your being.

Amidst the process of separation, breakdown, and expansion, there may be moments of ugliness and chaos, yet this formlessness is where God's transformative work thrives. As the Lord's voice fills the heavens and reaches the ends of the earth, so too shall He fill the voids in your life in this significant season of divine intervention. This is not a time for silence; it is a season to saturate your life with the words of God, embracing the new, the unknown, and the beautifully formless that He is birthing within you.

Rebuilding Foundations

In the process of breaking free from cycles that have long held you captive, God orchestrates multiple occurrences towards the end of your journey of liberation. What may seem like torture is, in truth, God's way of setting you free from the ruling spirit that has dictated your path. The influence of mothers, whether physical bearers or spiritual nurturers, plays a crucial role in guiding and shaping the next generation. Your wounds carry the potency to birth new beginnings—a legacy that must be safeguarded for the future.

Because of the need for transformation, there is an urgency for spiritual progression to a deeper knowledge of God and self. Accessing divine revelation hinges on walking in the Spirit, paving the way for reclaiming occupied lands of rejection and hindrances to promises. Rebuilding becomes essential as God uncovers the root of the issues, akin to the Babylonian exile as punishment for disobedience and idolatry.

It's time to keep going! And for some, it's time to begin! Don't let discouragement stop you—let it push you. Don't let rejection make you crawl back under the rock. Every time I would be rejected or feel rejected, I would stop what I was doing and make an excuse as to why I stopped, knowing that the root cause was rejection. Sometimes, because you're dealing with the spirit of rejection, your perception will be rejection, even when it's not. Rejection started when I was young, and it grew up with me, hiding itself for periods of time before rising up and gripping me along with fear right when I'm soaring in a certain area. Rejection makes you upset when people don't accept what you're doing. Do your purpose no matter what. Do it unto God. Yes, it hurts when you're not accepted, but do it because it's your passion, it's your purpose, and it's going to bless others to fulfill theirs. The devil will use any door to get you to stop, and if you willingly allow rejection or fear or any of its cousins to continue to rule your life, then you won't continue to progress or gain ground. I denounce rejection and fear right now in the name of Jesus. Be free and walk in your true identity and fulfill God's will for your life.

Sometimes the answer to our problems is right there, but we're too blinded by the past to see it. Listen, the change happens in you. Do you know that the issue you have in your life right now has way too much of your attention? It has you distracted. You have taken your eyes off of God, and now the issue, the person, whatever it is, is your God. You wake up worrying about it, you go to sleep worrying about it. When all God says to do is speak to it. Speak what, though? What does God say about stress? Does He say, "You go ahead and lose sleep over that hurt," or "You can give it to Me and work on the master plan of your life today and tomorrow"? Look in the mirror and tell yourself, "Your focus is off." Look to Him, give it to Him, and stay close to Him. And your life will make a major turn for the better. You're too heavy to pick up the torch of greatness because you're carrying the garbage from the past. So make room for what God has for you!

The cyclical nature of building, breaking down, and rebuilding stems from faulty foundations, leading to cracks and structural misalignment in our lives. The focus on laying a strong foundation, rooted in knowledge and divine wisdom, is emphasized as the key to enduring spiritual and personal growth. The repercussions of generational legacies, both beneficial and harmful, underscore the necessity of breaking down faulty foundations to pave the way for renewal and alignment with God's plan.

As the journey unfolds, it becomes evident that only by addressing the root causes and tearing down idols can true freedom and alignment with God's purpose be achieved. Through the rebuilding process, guided by divine revelation and spiritual alignment, individuals are empowered to break free from cycles of destruction and embark on a transformative journey toward wholeness and fulfillment.

BUILDING ALTARS: A PATH TO RENEWAL

Have you ever felt a warning from God of impending devastation, accompanied by tests and instructions for preparation? Just as Israel was forewarned through the prophet Jeremiah, they were advised to build, settle, seek peace, and pray amidst exile, knowing that restoration and prosperity awaited. Indeed, plans were in place to bring hope and a future, as revealed through Isaiah and the promise of rebuilding by Cyrus.

Before the foundation of the temple was laid, an altar was rebuilt as a place of sacrifice and separation—a point of spiritual strength and connection. David's desire to establish a permanent place of worship reflects the journey of inviting God's presence to dwell both within and among His people. In times of catastrophe, the greatest victories can emerge, as seen in David's costly mistake leading to repentance at Araunah's threshing floor.

Mount Moriah, the chosen temple site, holds significance as the place where Abraham was tested with the sacrifice of Isaac, emphasizing the weight of prayer and motives in divine alignment. Sacrifices, acts of separation, and offerings were pivotal components of renewing the relationship between humanity and the Holy God under the law.

While David's yearning to build the temple was deferred to Solomon, the preparation work laid the foundation for its eventual construction. Solomon's temple, though lasting for centuries, saw destruction and restoration, marking a journey of faith and resilience amidst trials. The evolution of the temple under Herod the Great, witnessing the teachings of Jesus and the apostles within its courts, signifies a spiritual and historical site of profound significance.

As the temple stands as a metaphor for spiritual regeneration and divine connection, the journey of rebuilding altars, both physical and metaphorical, underscores the importance of sacrifice, separation, and alignment with God's will. Through preparation, obedience, and offerings that come at a cost, the path to renewal and restoration unfolds, transforming devastation into opportunities for divine encounter and relationship. In the altars we build, may we find the strength, peace, and connection that lead to a deeper understanding of God's presence in our lives.

BUILDERS OF RENEWAL: THE RESTORATION OF FAITH AND THE TEMPLE

In the journey of rebuilding and restoring the temple, the roles played by Zerubbabel, Ezra, and Nehemiah stand out as pivotal in the narrative of faith and renewal.

The Israelites remained in Babylon for seventy years, and only after those seventy years in captivity were they allowed to return. They came back in three stages: under Zerubbabel, under Ezra, and under Nehemiah.

Zerubbabel, born in Babylon under Persian rule, heeded the call to rebuild the temple, supported by the endorsement of God's authority, signified by setting him as a signet ring.

After the foundation of the new temple was laid, challenges arose as the size paled in comparison to Solomon's grand structure, leading to discouragement among the people. However, the significance lies not just in rebuilding physically but in preparing spiritually for the restoration to be sustained and multiplied, urging a call to not settle for less than what God intends.

Ezra, a priest and scribe, embodied the essence of aid and protection in his return to Jerusalem from Babylon, fulfilling the prophecy of the end of captivity as decreed by Cyrus. His dedication to studying and teaching the law of the Lord exemplifies the importance of personal devotion and discipline in serving as a shepherd and minister in Jerusalem.

Cyrus' decree, influenced by God's touch on his heart through Jeremiah's prophecy, paved the way for the exiles to return to their position and rebuild the temple. The proclamation of freedom and restoration resonates with the fulfillment of God's word over one's life, echoing the readiness to shepherd the season well after enduring testing.

As the people prepared to build the house of the Lord in Jerusalem, the assistance from neighbors and the liberation of temple articles by King Cyrus showcased a collective effort toward restoring the divine presence within the temple walls. The unity in providing silver, gold, goods, and livestock for the temple underscored a communal dedication to the cause of rebuilding and renewing their faith.

In the interconnected journeys of Zerubbabel, Ezra, and Nehemiah, the restoration of the temple serves as a testament to the power of faith, dedication, and divine intervention in guiding the faithful towards a path of renewal, both spiritually and physically. Through their stories, we are reminded of the importance of heeding God's call, preparing diligently, and working together towards rebuilding what has been broken, ultimately leading to the restoration of faith and the fulfillment of divine promises.

BROKEN WALLS, RESTORED HEARTS: A JOURNEY OF EXILE AND REBUILDING

The concept of exile, being barred from one's native country, is not only physical but also deeply rooted in the spiritual, mental, and emotional realms. This exile often manifests as bondage to the old self, fear of embracing change, and reluctance to offend others by stepping into the abrasive truth. However, embracing the abrasive aspects of oneself is essential for growth, as reflected in the division brought by the sword of God's Word between truth and resistance.

God's call to stop replaying the old sad songs and instead embrace the restoration and rebuilding He offers is a transformative message. Zephaniah's words resonate with the promise of delight and joy in God's restoration process, emphasizing the importance of seeking intimacy and purpose over mere works.

Nehemiah's role as cupbearer to the king symbolizes trustworthiness, paving the way for him to lead the restoration of Jerusalem's walls. The permission, resources, and governorship granted to Nehemiah by King Artaxerxes enabled the rebuilding of the walls in just 52 days, fulfilling Daniel's prophecy of restoration in difficult times.

Nehemiah's encounter with the broken walls of Jerusalem mirrors the brokenness survivors of exile face, highlighting the need for restoration and defense against external threats. The broken walls and burned gates signify vulnerability and the critical condition of those returning from exile, mirroring the broken state of the world today.

Jeremiah's recount of the trouble and disgrace faced by survivors of exile underscores the critical state of affairs both in Jerusalem and the world. The broken walls serve as a poignant metaphor for defense, while the burned gates symbolize entry points that need protection and restoration.

In the midst of brokenness and exile, the call to rebuild, restore, and fortify becomes essential for survival and growth. Just as Nehemiah led the reconstruction of Jerusalem's walls, each individual is called to rebuild what has been broken and foster a protective environment amidst difficult times. Through the journey of exile and rebuilding, broken walls can serve as a reminder of the transformative power of restoration and the resilience found in rebuilding the foundations of faith, community, and identity.

Rebuilding with God's Power

The narrative of Zerubbabel's authority and power in rebuilding the temple resonates deeply with the significance of divine approval and empowerment in carrying out monumental tasks. In Haggai 2:23, God's declaration to Zerubbabel of setting him as a signet ring symbolizes not only His sovereign presence but also the bestowal of authority and power upon him. Through this act, the King of Kings grants Zerubbabel the necessary tools to lead the restoration project with divine backing.

The concept of the signet ring as a symbol of authority and power finds parallels in other biblical narratives. Pharaoh's gift of his signet ring to Joseph signifies the appointment of Joseph as second-in-command over Egypt, a position of great authority and influence. Similarly, in the book of Esther, King Xerxes entrusts Haman with his signet ring, granting him the power to issue a decree that threatens the Jewish people. The signet ring serves as a tangible representation of the king's authority and a seal of approval on significant decrees and decisions.

Drawing from these examples, the concept of the signet ring underscores the pivotal role of divine authority and power in significant moments of history. Just as Zerubbabel was entrusted with authority by God to oversee the rebuilding of the temple, Joseph and Haman wielded great power through the signet ring bestowed upon them by earthly kings.

The significance of God's authority and power in the process of rebuilding extends beyond physical structures to spiritual and emotional restoration. Through the symbol of the signet ring, believers are reminded of the unwavering support and empowerment granted by God to undertake transformative endeavors and face challenges with courage and conviction.

As we navigate our own paths of rebuilding, may we seek the divine signet of authority and power, knowing that with God's backing, we have all we need to overcome obstacles and bring restoration to our lives and communities. Just as Zerubbabel, Joseph, and Haman were entrusted with authority through the signet ring, may we embrace God's empowering presence in our journeys of renewal and transformation.

Prayer is our mirror, revealing how God sees us. The devil tries to hinder our prayer life because it exposes our true selves. Prayer is how we see ourselves, how God sees us, and how His will is revealed. It's how we're able to see the traps of the enemy, have the scales removed from our eyes, and hear more. Prayer is how we're able to break free from chains when we're in the presence of God, like a time capsule. God takes us back in time to show us the original plan, and then brings us back to our reality, revealing what we need to shift and bring into place to align with His plan. God doesn't reveal everything to us; He reveals it to all of His children, and we help each other get it together. Prayer is how we come together as one, working together with God's children to help each other get it together, and God gives prophecy in part. The devil wants to isolate us and keep us from knowing our true purpose, but God has someone connected to us who will counterattack the enemy's whispers. God is breaking down the false self that He did not ordain, and He's stripping away anything that stands in the way of His will being done. We need to strip away our false selves and come back to who God created us to be, just like rebuilding the altar before rebuilding the temple.

INTERACTIVE ACTIVITY

Identifying My Brokenness

1. What does brokenness mean to me? How do I experience it in my life? (Consider emotional, spiritual, relational, or physical aspects.)

_____

_____

_____

_____

_____

_____

_____

_____

_____

_____

_____

2. Describe a specific situation or period when you felt especially broken. (What happened? How did it make you feel?)

_____

_____

_____

_____

_____

_____

_____

_____

_____

_____

_____

_____

3. What are the emotions tied to this experience? (e.g. anger, sadness, fear, confusion, etc.)

_____

_____

_____

_____

_____

_____

_____

_____

_____

_____

_____

_____

_____

4. What insights or lessons have you gained from your experience of brokenness?

_____

_____

_____

_____

_____

_____

_____

_____

_____

_____

_____

_____

_____

5. Pray and for at least 10-15 minutes and allow God to speak to you about how to address these issues. Write down what was revealed.

_____

_____

_____

_____

_____

_____

_____

_____

_____

_____

_____

_____

_____

_____

_____

6. What are three specific areas of your life that you want to focus on for growth? (These could relate to emotional healing, relationships, career, etc.)

_____

_____

_____

_____

_____

_____

_____

_____

_____

_____

_____

_____

_____

_____

_____

7. For each area, list one or two actionable steps you can take in the coming days or weeks. (Make them specific and realistic.)

_____

_____

_____

_____

_____

_____

_____

_____

_____

_____

_____

_____

8. How can I incorporate support from others in these areas? (This could relate to seeking help from friends, joining a group, or finding a mentor.)

_____

_____

_____

_____

_____

_____

_____

_____

_____

_____

_____

6. Strategies for War
Demonic Attacks and Strongholds

The enemy's agenda is to kill, steal, and destroy, and this is often achieved through strongholds that hold us captive. A stronghold is an internal battle, where a malevolent force has gained significant influence in our lives and must be eradicated. The enemy's goal is to influence our lives, steal our anointing, and destroy our purpose.

How Strongholds Develop

Strongholds develop when we are unaware of our vulnerabilities and the access the demonic realm has to our minds. The attack comes, and the stronghold forms. The demonic influence seizes us, not with our consent but with legal right.

Breaking and Destroying Strongholds

To break strongholds, we must obey the Holy Spirit, becoming the altar —a place of sacrifice and separation. We need to be willing to surrender our old ways and receive new life from God. As we walk in authority and power, strongholds will be destroyed. The devil aims to distort what we hear by keeping us off the altar, affecting how we see things. Keep your fire burning at a high flame. The flame is God; if the devil comes close to you—the altar—he will be consumed by God.

"God is a refuge for the oppressed and a stronghold in times of trouble."

— PSALM 9:9

THE BATTLE

The battle is won or lost in the mind, where we believe, conceive, and take action. The enemy's weapons are mighty in God, used to pull down strongholds. It's in the mind that we believe, in the heart that we conceive, and in the spirit that we take action.

THE IMPORTANCE OF DISCERNMENT

Discernment is crucial in this spiritual fight. We need to know who God is to understand what we are fighting. We must ask questions and seek answers. If we don't discern the situation now, we will continue to follow others or situations until we face it head-on.

"For though we live in the world, we do not wage war as the world does. The weapons we fight with are not the weapons of the world. On the contrary, they have divine power to demolish strongholds. We demolish arguments and every pretension that sets itself up against the knowledge of God, and we take captive every thought to make it obedient to Christ. And we will be ready to punish every act of disobedience, once your obedience is complete."

— 2 CORINTHIANS 10:3-6

The Word of God in 2 Corinthians 10:3-6 reminds us that although we walk in the flesh, we do not war according to the flesh. The weapons of our warfare are not carnal but mighty in God for pulling down strongholds, casting down arguments, and every high thing that exalts itself against the knowledge of God, bringing every thought into captivity to the obedience of Christ, and being ready to punish all disobedience when our obedience is fulfilled.

THE KEY TO OVERCOMING

The key to overcoming demonic attacks and destroying strongholds is knowing God intimately—not just knowing of Him, but having a deep relationship with Him. 2 Corinthians 10:5 says, "We demolish arguments and every pretension that sets itself up against the knowledge of God, and we take captive every thought to make it obedient to Christ."

The devil wants to keep us off the altar so he can distort what we hear. But if we keep our fire burning at a high flame, he will be consumed by God. This is why we need to know God intimately and maintain that relationship. Without knowing God, we will never experience permanent change in our lives. We need to gain traction in the spirit because we often experience a spiritual surge that fades until the next gathering, which is why our lives produce little to no fruit.

Many times we feel the effects of war even when personal attacks haven't directly hit us; the impact on the one who hits the landmine is far greater than on those in the vicinity.

The true key to deliverance and maintaining it is keeping the doors closed. What are these doors? The gateways? If we access heaven and bring it to earth, hell's tactics can also access us without our knowledge, disrupting our flow. Are you in the flow of heaven or hell? People are so open to the spirit world. The Holy Spirit should be your gateway, controlling what comes in and out and flows through you. You can be someone's blessing or downfall by what you release. The Bible says out of your heart flow the issues of life. It's what comes out of a person that defiles them. Once it's released, it's manifested. This is why you must be mindful of what goes in so that what comes out will produce heaven.

We have to be fruitful, multiply, and replenish the earth. What are you filling the earth with? What fruit are you producing? Read and study the Word, and revelation will come. Get ready for the release.

What company do you keep? You become like those you surround yourself with. We can have a group of people, some of whom are leaders with strong leadership qualities, and others who simply go with the flow. Some people are naturally strong-willed and have dominant personalities, leading the group without even realizing it. This doesn't mean that person is better than others; it could be a natural trait God placed in them.

No matter what position you hold, you cannot let any group influence you into doing something outside of what God has called you to do. The people you surround yourself with will either propel you forward or cause you to take several steps back. You become the company you keep.

Others won't always see things the way you do. Choosing to follow Jesus is a choice, yes, but it's the best choice. Some of us are following things and people that will never benefit our future. These influences may not even know us and probably never will.

The world needs God—will you be His representative? He's in heaven on the throne, and He has us, His children, to represent Him, to gather our brothers and sisters, to come into the ark, to come into safety, to become who we were created to be.

This life is a race, whether we're running fast, jogging, or walking briskly—everyone is going at their own pace. But when you see track runners, they wear the lightest clothes and running shoes to stay light. We wake up heavy, go through our days heavy, and go to sleep heavy, carrying burdens that were never meant for us to carry.

One of our greatest enemies is worry. When you worry, you carry it like a baby in your womb. It's so deeply rooted that it spills into everything you do. This robs you of your drive and will to live a healthy and meaningful life. You can't give God your all or give life your best shot while carrying all this garbage.

Some things won't let you go easily because they've matured with you; they've become part of you. You may need help digging them out. You have help—ultimately from God—and from people who will pray with you and walk you through deliverance from anything that has you bound to the point that you can't live freely. Jesus died for our freedom —it's time to receive and embrace what was freely given to us.

There are two kinds of people in the world: those who will go and get it and those who are on the sidelines waiting for it to happen. God has called us to make it happen. He told the children of Israel that the land of Canaan was theirs—the Promised Land.

So, when you know that something belongs to you, what's stopping you from getting up and going after it? Do you know what it is? It's our mindset. How am I going to get it? Do I deserve it? Did God really say that?

This is your season to get what's yours. Come into full alignment with God's will so that you don't miss what He's trying to show you. You are not being punished; you just have to make some adjustments to be ready for what God has shown you is yours.

Do you believe God? We can't put our trust in man, the government, or the justice system more than or over what God says. The Bible says that the just shall LIVE by faith. Living by faith is not optional for those who walk with God. There will be times in our lives when we won't see with our natural eyes what we know God has said.

This is why we not only have to have faith but also walk and live in the spirit, meaning we are living by what God says alone. Faith brings what we are believing God for into reality. Faith is the evidence of things not seen, meaning it's the confidence that what I don't see yet *will happen*.

It is by faith that the world we exist in today was framed—it was framed by the Word of God. What have we spoken in our lives that framed our lives? We can blame things and people, but what have we spoken and acted on that became our reality lately and in years past?

I challenge you to believe and speak differently according to the Word of God. You can't speak what God knows if you don't know Him, so I challenge you to read the Word and watch it change your life!

Worship is the Key to the Release of God's Power

When God speaks, things transform. Read the following Scriptures in Psalms that attest to the power of God being released as a result of worshipping Him.

Psalm 63:1-8

1 You, God, are my God,
    earnestly I seek you;
I thirst for you,
    my whole being longs for you,
in a dry and parched land
    where there is no water.
2 I have seen you in the sanctuary
    and beheld your power and your glory.
3 Because your love is better than life,
    my lips will glorify you.
4 I will praise you as long as I live,
    and in your name I will lift up my hands.
5 I will be fully satisfied as with the richest of foods;
    with singing lips my mouth will praise you.
6 On my bed I remember you;
    I think of you through the watches of the night.
7 Because you are my help,
    I sing in the shadow of your wings.
8 I cling to you;
    your right hand upholds me.

Psalm 66:5-10

5 Come and see what God has done,
    his awesome deeds for mankind!
6 He turned the sea into dry land,
    they passed through the waters on foot—
    come, let us rejoice in him.
7 He rules forever by his power,
    his eyes watch the nations—
    let not the rebellious rise up against him.
8 Praise our God, all peoples,

let the sound of his praise be heard;
⁹ he has preserved our lives
   and kept our feet from slipping.
¹⁰ For you, God, tested us;
   you refined us like silver.

Psalm 71:14-24

¹⁴ As for me, I will always have hope;
   I will praise you more and more.
¹⁵ My mouth will tell of your righteous deeds,
   of your saving acts all day long—
   though I know not how to relate them all.
¹⁶ I will come and proclaim your mighty acts, Sovereign Lord;
   I will proclaim your righteous deeds, yours alone.
¹⁷ Since my youth, God, you have taught me,
   and to this day I declare your marvelous deeds.
¹⁸ Even when I am old and gray,
   do not forsake me, my God,
till I declare your power to the next generation,
   your mighty acts to all who are to come.
¹⁹ Your righteousness, God, reaches to the heavens,
   you who have done great things.
   Who is like you, God?
²⁰ Though you have made me see troubles,
   many and bitter,
   you will restore my life again;
from the depths of the earth
   you will again bring me up.
²¹ You will increase my honor
   and comfort me once more.
²² I will praise you with the harp
   for your faithfulness, my God;
I will sing praise to you with the lyre,

Holy One of Israel.
²³ My lips will shout for joy
    when I sing praise to you—
    I whom you have delivered.
²⁴ My tongue will tell of your righteous acts
    all day long,
for those who wanted to harm me
    have been put to shame and confusion.

The three Scripture references in Psalms (63, 66, and 71) emphasize the importance of seeking God, praising Him, and acknowledging His power. There is a deep longing to worship and praise God that releases His sustainability to us as His children. Are we thirsty for God to the extent that we should be to experience more of His glory? God is inviting us to come and see His works—are we in proximity to Him? Even in times of trouble and hardship, it is crucial to express gratitude for God's righteousness and salvation.

This is the key to more in our lives and every area. The adversary wants us to curse our situation with our own words out of frustration, but instead, we should praise, worship, and give God adoration. This opens us up to Him, allowing Him to fill that place of frustration with healing and wholeness.

THE POWER OF GOD

The power of God is the supernatural ability to do the miraculous. Supernatural means a force beyond scientific understanding and the laws of nature. When you allow your vision to consume your life and your entire being, you change, and so does everyone connected to you.

1. How else can someone die and come back to life?
2. How else can someone diagnosed as paralyzed from the waist down, and told they would never walk again, get up and walk?
3. How else can you get approved for a house, even when your credit score doesn't match the required status?

4. How else could it be that you call the dealership to make
   your monthly payment, and they say it's already paid in full?

The power of God is essential for salvation, as revealed in Romans
1:16, and is received through the Holy Spirit. This power is not just for
salvation but for daily living, strengthening our inner being (Ephesians
3:16), enabling us to serve (Ephesians 3:7), and empowering us in ways
beyond our natural abilities (Acts 3:6). We are empowered by God's
power to endure suffering (2 Timothy 1:7-8), and it is perfected in our
weakness (2 Corinthians 12:9). We find power in prayer (James 5:16),
and God empowers us for ministry, giving us the confidence to speak in
His name (Matthew 28:18-20). The power of God is beyond our
comprehension, working on our behalf to do far more than we can ask
or imagine (Ephesians 3:20), giving us everything we need for living a
godly life as we come to know Him (2 Peter 1:3).

The power of God increases as we develop spiritual maturity, recognizing that His power is working for us. Unfortunately, many of us lack
awareness of this power and its mechanics, leading to a lack of effectiveness in our lives. Imagine how much more we could achieve if we understood how to access all of God's power and provision! God wants us to
be aware that we have angelic assistance available to help us navigate
life's challenges, providing us with an unseen support system that can
amplify our abilities.

*"The angel of the Lord encamps around those who fear Him, and rescues
them."*

— PSALM 34:7

Angels are real and play a significant role in our lives, with each
person having an assigned angel to minister to their interests. We must
believe in their mission, which includes rescuing, protecting, and taking
over our battles, as well as strengthening us (Luke 22:43). When we
pray, we can make demands for angelic interventions and issue specific,
faith-filled commands for what we want them to do, just like Jesus did
in Matthew 26:53. Our angels are waiting on our orders and will only

deliver our instructions if we give them clear guidance. For example, Elisha instructed an angel to smite enemies with blindness, and they obeyed (2 Kings 6:17-18). To put our angels to work, we must refuse to be afraid, as fear can hinder their ability to deliver. Instead, we should keep saying what the Word says and trust in God's promises, even in the midst of adversity. This requires obedience, steadfastness, and consistency to flow in the power of God.

What Hinders the Power from Flowing:

1. Unforgiveness
2. Disobedience
3. Offense
4. Sin
5. Pride
6. Unbelief

Mark 9:24 says, "Jesus said to him, 'If you can believe, all things are possible to him who believes.' Immediately the father of the child cried out and said with tears, 'Lord, I believe; help my unbelief!'"

The power of God is not limited to a specific source, as seen in the case of Samson. Despite his misuse of power, Samson was still able to achieve great victories, judging Israel for 20 years and ultimately freeing the nation from Philistine oppression. However, his failure to keep his vows, including abstaining from wine and cutting his hair, led to a broken covenant and ultimately resulted in his downfall. The hair was not the source of Samson's power, but rather a part of his vow that he broke. Despite his flaws, God still worked through Samson's fleshly desires to accomplish His greater goals, showcasing His marvelous wisdom.

The power of God was demonstrated in the lives of King Uzziah and his son Jotham. Uzziah, who reigned for 52 years, built towers and fortified Jerusalem, demonstrating his wisdom and leadership. He also sought God during the days of Zechariah, and as long as he sought the Lord, God gave him success (2 Chronicles 26:5). However, when Uzziah became strong, his heart was lifted up to his destruction. He transgressed against the Lord by burning incense on the altar of incense, an act reserved for the priests (2 Chronicles 26:16). This mistake led to Uzziah's downfall, as he was stricken with leprosy and died. Similarly, Jotham, who reigned for 16 years, did what was right in the sight of the Lord, according to all that his father Uzziah did. He was a king who sought God and was given success. However, when we are honored or applauded, we must be careful not to get ahead of ourselves and do things that God did not call us to do.

The Breath of God gives life, but when our vision is dim, we may lack conviction and struggle to feel the presence of God. This can lead to repeated wounds that go unnoticed and unaddressed, resulting in a loss of vitality and extremities. However, there are two main things that can enforce the power of God in our lives: seeking Him (2 Chronicles 26:5) and preparation (2 Chronicles 27:6). These principles were exemplified by King Uzziah and King Jotham, who built towers, fortified them, dug wells, and expanded their territories. Jotham's greatest obstacle was his war against the king of the Ammonites, but it was through this challenge that he produced his greatest testimony. As Jotham walked steadfastly before the Lord, he grew powerful and became a mighty leader.

IT'S A PROCESS

Change doesn't happen overnight; it's an intentional seeking of God—a hunger after His righteousness. When He lives inside of us, we take on His character and nature, but the transformation is gradual as we seek Him, pray, and read the Word. It happens over time. There are many dynamics involved in the process of change. Sometimes we get frustrated when we don't see immediate changes, especially in things we've been praying about for a long time. But when we pray for change, God is also changing things within us. We may have our adult tantrums, asking God why we had this family, why we were raised this way, why we were abandoned as children, or why people don't respond to us like they do to others. Then we move into the "what ifs"—what if I never had a baby at 15, what if I never joined that gang, what if I was raised in a better neighborhood? We think that our lives would have turned out differently. But we can't determine our future based on the whys and what-ifs. That is bondage to guilt, shame, and regret, and we can't dwell on that and move forward.

God wants His standard raised back in the church and in our individual lives. A high standard can only be achieved through the Holy Spirit. Don't get caught up in what you can't do or how much you don't fit in with others; rather, focus on rising to God's standard. Remember, if God is for you, He is more than the world against you. Let's take a moment to pause and reevaluate everything. People will know that you have walked with God by the life that you live, not by how many people like what you're doing. Motives fluctuate with people. Our hearts are desperately wicked; who can know them? We don't even know what we are capable of doing, whether good or bad, because only God knows the depths of our hearts and beings. Let's stay close to God and reevaluate our "why." Make sure your 'why' lines up with the will of God for your life. God has an appointed time when things are going to happen. It's time to dream again! What do we do while we wait? *Wait means preparation*! We can't just throw God the scraps of our lives; we have 24 hours in a day—how much time is dedicated to seeking the Lord and spending time with Him? How much time do we invest in making sure we fulfill our purpose? How much time do we spend planning our future?

God says, "I'm coming after the hidden things." The devil will no longer sidetrack or ambush you ever again! God is pulling the covers off everything that has stopped you in the past; you will overcome it because you are an overcomer! You know that thing, that little thing you swept under the rug and tried to ignore, thinking you were okay? God says, "I'm pulling that from under the rug so that it won't lift its ugly head at the inopportune time when I'm trying to propel you to the next place."

God wants us to be overcomers—we can't serve two masters. We either love one and hate the other. There are only two choices: God or the devil. Who will you choose? We can't afford to detour and waste time in a place where we are not called to be. God is rooting it up. Enough is enough; it's coming up and out. Things have been planted along the way, watered, and have grown up right along with us. God is exposing it. Do you want to hold on to it and be stagnant, or let it go and be fruitful? We have to look at the patterns, pay attention to things happening over and over again, and break the cycle.

We have been going through our normal daily routine—going to work, coming home, running errands, maybe even being involved in ministry on some level. But God says there is more. Think about that particular idea you've had for years that you've never stepped out in faith to pursue. That's the dream God wants to awaken in you. He wants you to become aware of the opportunities He has for you in this new season of your life.

We have to delight ourselves in Him. *If we delight ourselves in Him, then He will give us the desires of our heart.* 'Delight' means to please greatly. Our lives should be so centered around doing God's will that whatever we ask, He knows it will be according to His perfect plan. God desires for us to succeed at home, in our church, in our community, in school, and in corporate America— just to name a few.

But what many of us fail to realize is that the verse doesn't say Jesus will do what we ask right now. None of us know God's timing or why it sometimes seems to take so much longer than we'd like. But we can rest in the truth that He is faithful.

INTERACTIVE ACTIVITY (PART 1)

Fill in the blank. The answer key is in the Appendix.

1. The object at hand isn't working properly, so we need to _____ concerning it to fix the problem.

2. When we take apart the system, we may find that there are other _____ leading up to the main issue.

3. God wants us to see the _____ work, not just what we see in the present moment.

4. The key to unlocking God's plan is receiving a _____ of who God is and our identity in Him.

5. According to John 10:27, God's sheep hear His _____ and follow Him.

Multiple Choice Questions

1. What is the main reason why we need to take apart the system to fix the problem?

    a) To see the big picture
    b) To identify the root cause
    c) To find a quick fix
    d) To avoid responsibility

2. What is the key to unlocking God's plan for our lives?

    a) Following our own desires
    b) Seeking guidance from others
    c) Receiving a revelation of who God is and our identity in Him
    d) Trusting our instincts

Reflection Questions

1. How do you think Peter's denial of Jesus affected his relationship with Jesus? What does this reveal about human nature and our tendency to deny or hide our true selves?

_____
_____
_____
_____
_____
_____
_____

_____
_____
_____
_____
_____
_____
_____
_____
_____
_____
_____
_____
_____

2. What does it mean to be "broken" and how can this lead to spiritual breakthroughs? Provide examples from your own life or experiences.

_____
_____
_____
_____
_____
_____
_____
_____
_____
_____
_____
_____
_____
_____
_____
_____

INTERACTIVE ACTIVITY (PART 2)

Fill in the blank. The answer key is in the Appendix.

1. The journey of rebuilding and restoration in the Bible is a powerful reminder of the importance of _____ , divine connection, and sacrifice.

2. The roles played by Zerubbabel, Ezra, and Nehemiah stand out as pivotal in the narrative of _____ and renewal.

3. The concept of exile is not only physical but also deeply rooted in the _____, mental, and emotional realms.

4. The signet ring symbolizes _____ authority and power.

Multiple Choice Questions

1. What is the significance of the signet ring in the biblical narrative?

    a) It represents earthly authority and power
    b) It symbolizes divine approval and empowerment
    c) It is a symbol of God's sovereignty
    d) It represents human creativity

2. What is the key to overcoming demonic attacks and destroying strongholds?

    a) Knowing God's will
    b) Knowing God intimately
    c) Knowing about God
    d) Knowing God's plan

3. What is the purpose of prayer in the Biblical narrative?

    a) To communicate with God
    b) To receive spiritual guidance
    c) To see oneself as God sees them
    d) To seek divine intervention

Reflection Question

How does the biblical narrative of rebuilding and restoration illustrate the importance of spiritual regeneration, divine connection, and sacrifice? There is no right or wrong answer. Please share your perspective.

_____
_____
_____
_____
_____
_____
_____
_____
_____
_____
_____
_____
_____
_____
_____
_____
_____
_____
_____

7. THE INDUCTION
OF THE NEW YOU
DECLARATIONS

According to the Oxford English Dictionary, 'induction' is defined as the action or process of introducing someone to a particular position or organization, such as the induction of a league into the Baseball Hall of Fame. It is also the process of bringing about or giving rise to a certain event or outcome.

> *"But we all, with unveiled face, beholding as in a mirror the glory of the Lord, are being transformed into the same image from glory to glory, just as from the Lord, the Spirit."*
>
> — 2 CORINTHIANS 3:18

> *"Beloved, we are God's children now, and what we will be has not yet appeared; but we know that when he appears, we shall be like him because we shall see him as he is."*
>
> — 1 JOHN 3:2

These two scriptures show us that to walk into the new realm we are in, it has to be revealed. It is not something we can figure out ourselves;

it can only be received in the spiritual realm. We are to become like Christ Jesus, as He bore our sins, insecurities, and struggles so that we can be transformed into His image.

For too long, many people have allowed circumstances to stop them from speaking up. But God gave us a voice, and our words have power! Let's fill the earth with the sound of victory! I got my voice back, and there are many people around the world who feel like they don't have a voice. They feel like their voice doesn't matter, and when they speak, no one is listening or hearing them. But God has given us a voice that creates sound—sound is airwaves, formed from words. Words create, words destroy, and words can cause things to crumble and fall. Words can also uplift and build. So, what will you use your words to do?

How do we know that words create? How do we know that words form? Let's go back to the beginning of time, where God, as the Father and Creator of all things, used His words to create the world and every-thing in it. Isn't that powerful? Did He or did He not give us a template for how to create the life He wants us to have? So, it seems to me that some of us need to shift our thinking and shift our language. Because most of the time, what you think about eventually becomes your speech. It's what you listen to that becomes your speech; it's what you watch that becomes your speech. And all of the things you listen to, and all of the things you watch, become your thinking, your mindset, and create your state of being—which determines your quality of life. So, if your life is not what you thought it would be, you have to change your language. If your life is not what God showed you it would be, you have to change your language. If you don't even know what your life is supposed to look like, you have to change your language and start talking to the One who knows how to create—that's God. Let's start reading the manual that shows us how to create—that's the Word of God; He is the living Word.

How did we receive this identity? Through Christ, not through education, not through man's approval, not through mistakes or flaws. Christ isn't flawed; there is no fault in Him. There is no pressure to be who He called you to be because to be is to let Him be. How easy is that? He said, "Let me live in you to help you walk out what we call purpose on earth through you." To bring others into the Kingdom where they belong. Coming out of an evil system into a freedom culture was specifically designed for you. You don't have to try to fit; you just fit. So you come out of falsehood into truth. The washing of the Word of God—the residue of the world will leave. The reason it's hard for believers to be free is because of the lack of the Word of God; the Word is truth, light, power, and that's the key to freedom. If we wash every day, there is no room for buildup. When you wash every day in the Word, you will be more convinced to believe the truth rather than the lie. One of the reasons why we are so up and down in our faith is because we feed our flesh and spirit, and both of them rule. So one day you're all in, and the next day you forget what you were walking in. Both parts are alive and feeding you. The Word illuminates; when the sun shines on the tree, photosynthesis takes place, and the tree is able to receive its nutrients to stay alive and produce.

The tree essentially sleeps over winter, similar to how some animals —such as bears, snakes, or squirrels—hibernate during the cold months. To do this, a deciduous tree sends most of its vital nutrients to the roots, where they are stored over the winter. Photosynthesis is the process by which green plants and some other organisms use sunlight to synthesize foods from carbon dioxide and water. Photosynthesis in plants generally involves the green pigment chlorophyll and generates oxygen as a byproduct.

The transformative power of God's presence in believers is similar to how plants undergo a transformation through photosynthesis, receiving nourishment and growth from the sun. Believers can experience a transformation through their relationship with God, receiving spiritual nourishment and growth that was afforded to us through the Son—Jesus Christ.

To know who you are and that your identity is not defined by your past but by what God already created you to be. Who you are isn't based on what you get or waiting on what you want. God is and will remain who He is, and we are who He said we are, with or without all of the extremities. You came into the world naked, with nothing on you, yet the essence of who you are is in Him. Who are you? What is your purpose in life? Why do you exist? What does God say about a person's greatest fulfillment? What does God intend as your response to His work of grace and salvation on your behalf? Where do you find your place in God's story?

Identify your purpose based on Scripture. Focus more on "being" than on "doing." (Your purpose clarifies who God has shaped you to be. Understanding who God made you to be will prepare you to discover and pursue God's vision for your life.) Use language that grips and energizes you.

Read and declare these scriptures daily until you believe who God created you to be:

1. A new creation in Christ:

Therefore, if anyone is in Christ, he is a new creation; the old has passed away, and see, the new has come!"

— 2 CORINTHIANS 5:17

2. A child of God:

"But to all who did receive him, he gave them the right to be children of God, to those who believe in his name."

— JOHN 1:12

3. A branch of the true vine:

"I am the vine; you are the branches. The one who remains in me and I in him produces much fruit, because you can do nothing without me."

— JOHN 15:5

4. A friend of Jesus:

"I do not call you servants anymore, because a servant doesn't know what

his master is doing. I have called you friends, because I have made known to you everything I have heard from my Father."

— JOHN 15:15

5. Justified and redeemed:

"They are justified freely by his grace through the redemption that is in Christ Jesus."

— ROMANS 3:24

6. An heir:

"We are God's children, and if children, also heirs—heirs of God and coheirs with Christ—if indeed we suffer with him so that we may also be glorified with him."

— ROMANS 8:17

7. A sanctified saint:

"To the church of God at Corinth, to those sanctified in Christ Jesus, called as saints, with all those in every place who call on the name of Jesus Christ our Lord—both their Lord and ours."

— 1 CORINTHIANS 1:2

8. A temple of the Holy Spirit:

"Don't you know that your body is a temple of the Holy Spirit who is in you, whom you have from God? You are not your own."

— 1 CORINTHIANS 6:19

9. A member of Christ's body:

"Now you are the body of Christ, and individual members of it."

— 1 CORINTHIANS 12:27

10. An ambassador for Christ:

"Therefore, we are ambassadors for Christ, since God is making his appeal through us. We plead on Christ's behalf: 'Be reconciled to God'."

— 2 CORINTHIANS 5:20

11. The righteousness of God:

"He made the one who did not know sin to be sin for us, so that in him we might become the righteousness of God."

— 2 CORINTHIANS 5:21

12. Chosen:

"For he chose us in him, before the foundation of the world, to be holy and blameless in love before him."

— EPHESIANS 1:4

13. Adopted:

"He predestined us to be adopted as sons through Jesus Christ for himself, according to the good pleasure of his will."

— EPHESIANS 1:5

14. Redeemed and forgiven:

"In him we have redemption through his blood, the forgiveness of our trespasses, according to the riches of his grace."

— Ephesians 1:7

15. Sealed with the Holy Spirit:

"In him you also were sealed with the promised Holy Spirit when you heard the word of truth, the gospel of your salvation, and when you believed."

16. Made alive in Christ:

"But God, who is rich in mercy, because of his great love that he had for us, made us alive with Christ even though we were dead in trespasses. You are saved by grace!"

— Ephesians 2:4-5

17. Raised and seated with Him in the heavenly places:

"He also raised us up with him and seated us with him in the heavens in Christ Jesus."

— Ephesians 2:6

18. God's workmanship:

"For we are his workmanship, created in Christ Jesus for good works, which God prepared ahead of time for us to do."

— Ephesians 2:10

19. A citizen of heaven:

"But our citizenship is in heaven, and we eagerly wait for a Savior from there, the Lord Jesus Christ."

— PHILEMON 3:20

20. No longer a slave, but free:

"For freedom, Christ set us free. Stand firm then and don't submit again to a yoke of slavery."

— GALATIANS 5:1

GOD IS GIVING YOU YOUR VOICE BACK

For years, I kept silent due to my lack of confidence, not knowing who I was and who God had established me to be before I was formed in my mother's womb. Life is a journey of development, and experiences teach us how to navigate through it. Just like surviving on an island, we discover hidden strengths and abilities that were predetermined factors within us. But for me, healing began when I started demanding that my voice be heard. It was sparked by the removal of shame, guilt, and regret. I realized that God's love and the finished work of the Cross had already forgiven me, loved me, and chosen me. Now, I sense that God is saying to the world: it's time to step back and see the big picture; time is moving, and we can't waste valuable time waiting for a feeling or a big bang.

Suddenly, we'll see tidal waves of promotion in the spirit realm that were not humanly possible. God is looking for people consumed with Him, not just pursuing Him for tangible things but for those things that are eternal. He wants us to understand that our methods are temporal and not eternal; only when they are eternal will they be effective. As we connect with God, He awakens our inner potential, releasing the power that has been stored within us. It's time to stop waiting for a feeling or a big moment and start trusting in God's plan. The time is now to unleash our inner potential and step into the promotion that God has ordained for us.

YIELDING TO GOD'S POWER

God wants every area of your life yielded to Him because He knows that the devil will exploit any vulnerability to conquer the rest of your life. The devil will choose the area that is most vulnerable, but remember that God's strength is made perfect in our weakness, and His grace is sufficient. Let the weak say, "I am strong." We are more than conquerors through Christ Jesus. No weapon formed against us shall prosper.

These are not clichés, but the truth! We're not fighting with Nerf guns, using our natural defenses. God said, "Just use me as your defense." You win with God every time. Don't look at the bad things that happen in your life as all bad; rather, see them as an opportunity to learn and grow through the school of life. God will change your perspective, and you will understand why you had to go through something in a particular way. His ways are not our ways. Sometimes, it's good to think of it as God teaching you something out of what you're dealing with now. No, He's not purposely making things happen to teach you a lesson. But as you go through life, things will happen, and you will learn how to maneuver through it with God.

The Word of God is our weapon because when we read it, it washes us from our old mindset and transforms us into what God wants us to be. The Word is our x-ray machine, our MRI; it goes in and does the work sometimes without us even knowing. The Word is God Himself. The words we're reading are being embedded in our hearts, minds, souls, and spirits. We become it; it becomes us. When we know the Word, we know God, and when we know God, we benefit from the relationship—it's no longer one-sided. The Holy Spirit translates the logos, the written word, into rhema, the direct word for us. We will hear God because we have read His Word, and He can now translate what He needs us to know personally for our life specifically.

BREAKING FREE FROM THE PAST

God doesn't want us to stay stuck in low-level things and not come up to where He is to see things for what they really are. He wants us to know that in Him, we are greater and better than what we're facing. That's why He says, "Give it to Him." God has removed our transgressions from us, so let's *let it go*! It's time to get to know the powerful you that you don't know yet. The devil is afraid of the you that you don't know yet.

When it's time for you to come forth, God will have a midwife in place to help you walk this thing out called life. You need help, and it's okay to admit that you need help and accept it when it comes. We need to cut the umbilical cord— everything that's connecting us to our past, including generational connections, addiction, premature death, unsuccessful marriages, rejection, fear, abandonment, and unforgiveness.

God is unlocking our future, and everything that was locked up in our life is being unlocked. Some things that can keep our future captive are our own words, words spoken by others, covenants with people from our past, and soul ties. God is releasing us from it all. Receive this by faith, denounce the things that have connected us, read the Word daily, and revelation knowledge will flow. God will begin to reveal to us personally and through others the things that have given legal access to our lives. We must be willing to face the truth and let go of the past. We can't keep living in bondage to our past mistakes or circumstances. It's time to break free and move forward into the plans that God has for us.

RAISING THE STANDARD

God wants His standard raised back in the body of Christ, as well as in our individual lives. A high standard that can only be achieved through the Holy Spirit. We must stop getting caught up in what we can't do or how much we don't fit in with others, and instead focus on coming up to God's standard. Remember, if God is for us, He's more than the world against us. So, let's take a moment to pause and reevaluate everything. What's our why? Why do we do what we do? Is it because it's our purpose, the reason why we're here, ultimately to please God, to lead people to Christ, to leave a legacy, or to make an impact on the earth?

Our motives may fluctuate with people, but our hearts are desperately wicked, and only God knows the depths of our hearts and being. Let's stay close to God and reevaluate our why. Make sure our why lines up with the will of God for our life. When we take in the goodness of God, we release that. When we take in garbage, we release that, too. What are we feeding our spirit? What we feed ourselves, we will reproduce, and others will feed off of it.

The Bible tells us in Genesis that man was created to be fruitful and multiply and replenish the earth. One plants the seeds, another waters, and God gives the increase. What are we sowing, planting, watering, and who is in our garden monitoring it? What are the determining factors influencing what we produce? These answers determine how we live our lives and who we will choose to be the head over our lives.

We can't serve two masters. We either love one and hate the other. There are only two choices: God or the devil. Who will you choose? We can't afford to detour and waste time in a place where we are not called to be. God is rooting it up. Enough is enough; it's time to come up and out. Things have been planted along the way, watered, and have grown up right along with us. God is exposing it. Do you want to hold on to it and be stagnant, or let it go and be fruitful?

We have to look at the patterns, pay attention to things happening over and over again, and break the cycle. It was not meant for us to stay in the place we have been in for years without any major movement... as long as a plant is being fed, it will grow. Who and what is feeding us will determine our forward movement. Let's reevaluate, reposition ourselves, and make some decisions with the guidance of God that will change the scope of what we're about to walk into in this new season.

THE TIME IS NOW

It's crunch time. Do you feel that urgency, that pressure to push? We're called to push past the resistance to fulfill our purpose. In prayer, I heard the Lord say, "Don't waste any more time. Go now, plan now, go back to school now, pray now, seek God now, sign up for that course now, register that business now, start that ministry now." What are you waiting for? Prepare now for what's next.

We're praying for more, but are we ready to handle more? God wants us to steward well what we already have, and that calls for discipline with our time, money, family, school, job, and relationships—every area of our lives. We want an upgrade in every area, and we have to steward well and shift when it's time. And the time is now.

We can't keep repeating cycles. You were built to carry the glory of God, and your capacity to receive is being expanded. But first, let God dig out the junk. Make room for God in your life by removing every lie. It all comes down to what you believe. Make room for what God really intended for you. He's digging out unforgiveness, addiction, lack of discipline, procrastination, jealousy, pride, loneliness, unawareness of identity, low self-esteem, suicide, murder, lying, and replacing them with love, forgiveness, joy, peace, patience, wholeness, healing, a new heart, a heart to serve—and so much more.

Yesterday is gone, and today is a new day with new possibilities that will become your reality. You are more than enough. There will be no more lack in your life because it's not in Him. There is an abundant supply of all that you need in God. You can ask, and it shall be given; seek, and you will find; knock, and the door will be opened.

Some of us haven't even started the conversation with God because we're scared to approach Him. We're not sure if He hears us or if He's listening. We're not sure if there is a God, if He exists, or if He cares about us because our present situation hasn't seemed to change yet. Change has to happen within first, and it starts in the mind.

THE FAITH TO BELIEVE

When we first start to believe that God is God and that there is no failure in Him, we will know that He will never fail us. When we understand that God's love for us is not based on what we do or don't do, we will realize that there is no punishment in His love.

God's love is unconditional, rooted in His nature and character. When God created us, He gave us dominion over the earth. We can pray the Word of God concerning His promises, knowing that they will align with His will. We must remember that He is looking for covenant rela-tionships—we are His children, commissioned to change the world by spreading the good news. So, yes, He will supply all of our needs, but we are also charged to be as He is and to represent Him.

As we walk in this faith, we declare in the name of Jesus that you will go forth and produce everything that God purposes you to do on earth. We ignite the flame in you by the power of the Holy Spirit, may your hunger for God increase. At God's deliverance, you shall live and fulfill the purpose God has invested within you.

Let us break free from self-sabotage and destruction and allow God's purpose and plan for our lives to be fulfilled. We are not limited by what we can do or achieve; we are limited only by our own faith and obedience to God's will.

The Power of New Beginnings

As we reflect on the past year, it's easy to feel like we've been stuck in a rut. We make those New Year's resolutions at the beginning of the year, but often, to no avail; we find ourselves saying, "One more year, and I've failed again."

But what if I told you that God is not punishing us but rather empowering us to take control of our lives? When we understand that God has given us dominion over the earth, we realize that we have the power to command our harvest to come now. He promises to supply all our needs, and when we follow His timing, things will align with what He has said. We often forget that God is looking for covenant relation-ships, and we are His children, commissioned to change the world by spreading the Good News. As we remember this, we'll be charged to be like Him and represent Him. It's getting ready to happen, but it's up to you.

If you follow God's timetable, everything will flow according to His timing. As we enter this new season of life, I want to remind you that change is inevitable. Seasons change, and everything changes, but is the change intentional? You can live here with no goals, but change will still happen; it just may not be purposeful or aligned with your divine purpose.

So, do you want change? You have the power through God to produce change; it happens within and flows outward. It happens in you and changes everything around you. And I know what you're thinking— but how? The answer is simple: prayer.

Pray and ask God for strategy. The work gets done in prayer; prayer is an open portal for Heaven to be translated to earth. As we give God the best part of our day—our undivided attention—we will discover our true purpose and walk into the best days of our lives. These two words had been resonating in my heart for a couple of months: *new beginnings*! This life that you are about to unpack will spark something new in you — something that you haven't seen before.

As we embark on this new journey, I want to share more with you about a powerful truth that has transformed my life, and that is prayer. Prayer shows you what's next, reveals the point of it all, and gives you the big picture. It shows you who to connect with, who to separate from, what to do, when to do it, why things are happening, how to stop what's hindering you, and how to maintain what's being released. This concept has been instrumental in my life, and I'm excited to share it with you.

I've learned that when we give God the best part of our day—our undivided attention—we can overcome even the most daunting challenges. We can develop a "give it to God" mentality, just as I did when I felt overwhelmed by situations that seemed hopeless. When we surrender to God, we can experience immediate breakthroughs, and sometimes He walks us through a process to work out our issues and prepare us for the change.

Giving God the best part of our day is crucial. It's not about giving Him the scraps of our day when we're tired and worn out. It's about giving Him our refreshed and alert selves, our undivided attention. This is how we can truly experience the power of God in our lives. As we navigate this journey of self-discovery, it's essential to remember that God is sealing the deal on many things in our lives. Our time is now. When all of God's plans for us unfold, we'll be amazed at what He has in store for us.

In Deuteronomy 28:2, we're reminded that obedience is the key to receiving all that God has for us. When we obey God's will for our lives, we can experience all the blessings He has in store for us. As we move forward, I want to encourage you to receive these blessings by faith, knowing that your time is now. The world doesn't even know how blessed it will be when you release what's in you. When you give what you have back to God and He blesses it, get ready for something explosive! The power of God is attractive, and whatever you're trying to do that was once hidden is about to get exposure! So, watch it happen and share your testimony. You are getting ready to walk into the best days of your life because of your discovery of yourself through your relationship with God.

We, sometimes, find ourselves saying, "I want to believe you, God, but I just don't know if things will ever change. I have been waiting for a long time but haven't seen the transformation I was hoping for." Today, I want you to focus on the small victories along the way. It can be very distracting to get frustrated because the final result hasn't manifested yet. While you're waiting on the results, I want you to understand that it's not just about getting what you prayed for. It's about growing in the process, becoming more like God and who He created you to be on earth. Do you know that because He's God, He can do anything whenever He wants? But He is transforming you in the process to have faith in Him, yes, but also to do your part. You will cause things to happen in your own life because the residue of what has stopped you before will no longer have any weight in your life. You will be the change that the world and your situation need to produce that finale that you prayed about. It's not just about it happening; it's about who you become in the process.

COMMANDING YOUR HARVEST

As we navigate this journey of faith, I want to encourage those who may be feeling frustrated because they don't see the fruit of their labor. You have been sowing seeds for a long time, and you're saying to yourself, "Where is the harvest?" Let me tell you that you have the power to command your harvest to come now. God will supply all your needs according to His riches in glory. Just like a child who automatically knows that their parent is going to provide a place for them to live, food for them to eat, and clothes for them to wear, it's an automatic dependence that they have developed. These are promises in the Word of God that God is going to stay true to. But there is a rising confidence that God is building in you in this season. Will you command for a thing to be, and will it come into alignment with God's will for your life?

Not every path we take will be a bed of flowers and roses; sometimes, there will be thorns and thistles. Do we run from our calling because of the pain, or do we allow God's grace and mercy to soften the blow? God is our healing balm, our counselor, protector, and defense. We are greater than the struggles and challenges that we face. Take a moment to think back on some things that you have faced in life that you had no idea you would survive. But you are here today. Why? Because it is through God's power and angelic assistance that we are able to press through. Press through and live. Make an impact while you are here. Give someone a word of encouragement. Do you know that just one word from God can save someone's life? Don't be selfish, swallowed up in your own troubles, and fail to release what God placed in you to help the nation, your family, your community, your coworkers, your friends—whoever you come in contact with should encounter God because you have allowed Him to fill you with Himself.

I challenge you today to push past how you feel and release what God has placed inside of you. What God has given you is not a secret; it can no longer be hidden or kept in a safe. Some of you are waiting for the right time to be who God has called you to be. But I'm here to tell you today that the time is now. You can no longer contain what God has given you to produce on earth. It is overgrown; it is overdue. The pressure that you feel right now is the pressure to release all of the goodness of God that He placed inside of you. This precious investment is too costly to waste. You cannot keep silent in this season. You cannot retreat in this season; you cannot fall back in this season. It is time to break out. You cannot allow people, situations, or circumstances to stop you. When whatever you do becomes God-centered, you can never be stopped.

THE POWER OF GOD'S PLAN

Some people may not understand why we move the way we do. The Bible says that the steps of the righteous are ordered by God. It's God's divine plan at work for those who have committed their lives to the Lord to walk in His predetermined purpose. Even before you knew or understood God and His existence, He sent messengers (angels) to guide you. God used people to provide insight so that you wouldn't stray too far off track. Sometimes, we don't need to know all the details; all we need to know is that on the other side of this, we have victory. God is going to fulfill His investment in you. However, we can't live recklessly and expect God's plan to be on time and on schedule. His plan is perfect on its own; all He asks is that you yield to it and follow through. His plan will work to our benefit and to benefit others—it's a win-win situation.

One of the core issues that stops us from moving forward in many areas of our lives is poor planning. Many of us have groundbreaking ideas and visions with the potential to be great successes, but we refuse to sit down, write them down, and plan them out. God wants you to succeed; He gave you the vision for success. However, with vision comes opposition. Preparation requires focus and determination. There are so many things that try to rob us of our time. Before we know it, half the day is gone, and little to nothing is accomplished because we didn't plan properly. I want to challenge you to plan your days for the next three days. You have the time; make the time. Don't waste any more time.

God is moving suddenly in this season, which is why you have to watch what you say. If you haven't had a chance to hear my video about calling forth your harvest, go and listen to the replay. This year, especially in the last couple of months, I have experienced answered prayers as quickly as I prayed them. And all I hear God say is, "I heard you." I feel like getting out of my truck and running because it's not as though God doesn't want to move on your behalf. But He is saying to you today, "You're too quiet." You're talking about your problems to the wrong people; you're complaining about what's not happening instead of commanding what should be happening. There is a prerequisite to God releasing what He promised—He wants your heart; He wants you to live a life dedicated to Him. It's like giving a child a gold treasure, but they mishandle it because their heart isn't renewed. When you have God's heart, He can trust you with what He promised. It's about maturity; are you responsible enough to handle what you're praying for? You want higher positions in the company, you want to own the business, you want money to finance your visions—but do you have a plan? So God says, "Position yourself." Let Him prepare you for the suddenlies that He wants to give you. God can do it right now, but are you ready? He said, "Get ready!"

KNOWING YOUR PURPOSE AND ANOINTING

What are you called to do? Do you know what you are anointed to do? We have the ability to do many things, but what are you anointed to do? The anointing breaks every yoke of bondage. This is why it's important to know what you're called to do, and the anointing to do it will follow. When you lead a consecrated lifestyle, the anointing will follow. You can do many things, but is it delivering anyone? Is it changing anyone's life? You will flourish in what you're called to do.

Are you tired of waking up feeling like there's more to life than this? Well, you don't have to feel that way anymore. Listen, I know a lot is going on in the world, and sometimes you may think to yourself, "What's the use? Why try to achieve anything?" Is it worth it when the world seems to be getting worse? Remember, our sole responsibility is to share the gospel—the good news—with others who don't know that they have hope in Jesus Christ. God loved us so much that He gave His Son to die for us so that we can be free, saved, and preserved from the evil in this world, and so that we can have eternal life with God after this life, living forever in the New Heaven and New Earth where evil will be no more.

So, yes, we can still thrive in chaos and let others know that they can too. Until it's time to cross over, make the best of the time that God has given you. He didn't create you to be miserable; He created you to have an abundant, full life—not absent from trouble, but with peace in the chaos, knowing that whatever is meant to harm you will always work out for your good. So, go and be great, and make this life count. God will help you build the life that He planned for you. Do you know that you are God's masterpiece? Anything anyone says contrary to that is a lie. And why are you believing someone who had nothing to do with your destiny, even if that someone is your own thoughts? Stop lying to yourself in order to walk in truth. To walk in truth, you have to tell the truth about yourself. Who are you? Do you know? Do you know that if you really knew who you were, you would not be walking in a false life that wasn't even designed for you? Do you know that your life would be better if you really knew how God sees you? Before you even lived your life, He knew and saw how great you are and the potential you have. He said, "Only if you follow Me." It's not a quick fix; it's not a temporary thing; it's not something you can create on your own strength and tear down tomorrow. What God does is permanent, and you will always see results with what He promised you.

BREAKING FREE AND RECEIVING INCREASE

God says, "Just break out!" Imagine being in a jail cell with your hands and feet bound, but the door is open. This means you have the ability to walk right out of the situation, but the missing element is that your hands and feet are bound. That's the part God wants to address. He wants you to be truly free. You might say, "Lord, I want to be free indeed," and He responds, "Receive your freedom." Freedom is available —it's free. The struggle that has been debilitating you for a while now— it's time to be free from it.

God's purpose for you is to succeed. He told me to share with you four words: increase, release, rebuild, and restore. God is getting ready to add to your life, but you have to release the old to Him. That life you built with your own strength has to be torn down so that God can rebuild you and give you the life He originally intended for you. He will restore the cares of this life that have depleted your joy and peace. Not only will God restore, but He will also add to it. You will be greater than before. Everything is shifting in the world. Inflation is through the roof, and many people are worried and losing hope. But I'm reminded that in the Bible, Israel increased when Pharaoh tried to stunt their growth and make life harder for them. How much more will God do for us in this era?

Have you become so accustomed to dealing with a situation that it has become your norm? Do you start claiming it as yours? But in reality, it's something that is happening to you at the moment, but it's not yours. The present thing that you see right now does not have to be your reality. Your narrative is changing, and you are writing a new script to your story. What does your story sound like? What you keep hearing and seeing is not it. There has to be another plot to the story. You know how in movies something happens in the middle or towards the end that you didn't expect—it changes the outcome of the story. The plot is about to change. You won't have the same people in it. Look for changes in your appearance, your actions, even your locations. God is moving some of you physically from where you live to another place. Some of you are going back to school. Some are taking new paths in your careers. Some are getting ready to get married and start a family. Some are starting that mentorship program you've been dreaming about.

Unlocking Your Potential

As we embark on this journey of spiritual growth, let's begin by acknowledging that nothing God wants to do in our lives can be deemed small or insignificant. Imagine waking up every morning knowing that you are pleasing God and walking in your purpose. You are significant; you were made to change the world. I remember the story of the woman at the well—Jesus simply told her there was a better way of living, more beneficial than the life she was already living. After that encounter with Jesus, she couldn't contain herself; she went and told a whole town of people. The word got out that Jesus knows your name, everything about you, and can turn things around for your good.

There are many benefits to walking with God. He will do many things for you because that's what He promised. But have we ever asked God, "Lord, what can I do for you?" Well, I'm glad you asked. Two things: 1. Allow Him to be Lord over your life by accepting Jesus Christ as your Savior and King, receiving all the benefits of being a child of God, being born again, and being in the kingdom of God. 2. When you know Him, you know your purpose, you know what you are supposed to look like and sound like because you were made to be a reflection of Him, created in His image.

As we walk with God, let's make sure to show gratitude. Give thanks in all circumstances, for this is God's will for you in Christ Jesus. So no matter what you see happening right now, thank God because it will get better. Remember that godliness with contentment is great gain. We brought nothing into the world, and we can take nothing out. But if we have food and clothing, we will be content with these. Psalm 84:11 says no good thing will He withhold from those who walk uprightly. Let's draw close to God and stay with Him. You always win with Him; you're always protected with Him, always at peace. And you will never fail.

God is getting ready to release what you have been praying for, but He has to get your heart posture right. No matter what comes or goes, you stay with God. As we move forward, I encourage you to consider that your future is far beyond what you see right now. "Good" is not just a word; it's a word that God used to describe you. Something that He made is good, which means there is no flaw in you through His eyes. Let's break the cycle of pain, unforgiveness, past wounds, broken hearts, offense—the list goes on. It's time to get to the root of what's been holding you back. You shall move forward.

Did you know that you can activate your blessing by your faith and speaking God's word? God has already finished the work. Accept it, walk in it, and *own it— it's yours!* No more speaking the same negative words over your life. Let the four winds blow in every area of your life! Pray, plan, plant, and produce! As we continue on our journey of spiritual growth, we must understand that God is not just a God of the past, but also a God of the present and future. He is always working to bring forth His plans and purposes for our lives.

In this section, we will explore the ways in which God is working to bring about breakthroughs and advancements in our lives. God is going to give you now what you need for later. He is going to tend to your garden, nurturing seeds that have been planted by others and causing them to manifest. Your vision, purpose, love, peace, business, ministry, renewal, salvation, regeneration, deliverance, and healing are all unfolding now. But God has to root up some things that can't go with you to the next place. These takeaways from your life may not feel good, but they don't mean you any good. Yes, God will work it out for your good, but when things are being stripped from you, embrace the breaking away. You will understand it in time.

Sometimes our lives can be too cluttered with the wrong things that are not supposed to be there. God said if you only knew what He really had for you, you would not keep settling for less than your value. You are valued by how you see yourself. Our spiritual islands need to be cleared out to see our future only as God sees it. This is when you will manifest what God said about your life because you will live it, speak it, breathe it, believe it, and walk in confidence and boldness according to what God said. God is giving you the grace to finish and finish strong. Write down your goals and check them off as they are completed. This is how quickly God is going to redeem the time. You couldn't have planned what God is getting ready to release in your life if you tried. You will set a goal and finish in heaven's record time because this is what you were made to do.

We limit ourselves, but there are many gifts that we are given. Don't bury your gift; there are many sectors in you that have yet to be tapped into. And remember, He is the one who navigates and orchestrates this operational plan. Dedicate it back to Him, and this time it will be effective! It will produce and yield its fruit. Don't stop beginning! Make use of this valuable time that God has given us in this dispensation. Spend more time with the Father, and He will give direction on what and how to release what's in you! You will give birth! It's coming forth!

God says, "I heard you and I hear you." We often say we trust God, but do we really? He wants you to understand that He's got you. Being accepted into the family of God through His son Jesus through salvation is the best choice you could ever make, and it was the only choice on the table before sin came into the world. So God's divine plan is the best plan and the only option that works in our favor.

So yes, you have benefits for being a kingdom citizen, God's chosen, God's children. You may not believe this right now, but I'm a living witness that before you can even get it out of your mouth, God has a resolve. The power is in the spoken word of God. God said in the beginning, "Let there be," and there was. So according to God's plan and will for your life, this needs to be your new language: *"Let there be!"*

EMBRACING YOUR PURPOSE

You were made to change the world. The part that you play in God's masterpiece is important. When God wanted to deliver His people, Moses was born, Joshua was born, Jeremiah was born, and now you—do you know that your birthdate was not by chance? You were born when you were born to do what you are doing right now. Keep going, don't stop. At that moment when you feel overwhelmed, God will send angelic assistance. When Jesus was led up to the wilderness by the Holy Spirit to be tempted by the devil, God knew that the enemy's tactics wouldn't prevail. God wants to show you what you have—you have the willpower, the determination, and the grace to do what God has called you to do. Don't be afraid to begin; it's time to start. I'm going to pray. One of the signs of growth in any area is that you respond differently than before. Sometimes in life, we try to avoid difficult situations, thinking that if we don't touch them, they won't come up. But God doesn't want us walking on eggshells concerning life on any level. As much as we try to avoid the inevitable, it may show up at your doorstep, but how will you respond?

For a change in response, you have to get to work. First things first, no more denial about where you stand with it; if it hurts, it's okay to admit it. But you can't push it under a rug and expect things to change on their own. We have to be intentional about our change. Do you want change? Nothing will separate you from God's love. God's love covers and protects you. God wants to bring you to your expected end.

It's always God; every good and perfect thing comes from Him. You want to walk into the doors of blessings healed and whole. Did you know that you can open a door of blessing and not receive it because of that unresolved place in your heart? Declare it out of your mouth: "I will not allow depression to stop me, anxiety will not stop me, rejection will not stop me." You start declaring now what you have knowledge of. Type it or say it out loud: "I will not allow it; I will not allow."

No more! That situation has no more access to interrupt your life.

No more interruptions! It may try, but it will no longer stop your flow. Expect the change, embrace the change, walk in the change! God is getting ready to remind you of what He said. Sometimes life can distract you from what God promised. The pain can sometimes take your focus off of God's original plan. But I want you to keep living, keep going, keep praying, keep producing. You won't be left behind or forgotten. Lord, remind me, Lord, refresh my memory. Nothing can block what God purposed. Everything is being exposed! There are so many people in the world, and God hasn't forgotten about you. He's so powerful; He's meeting all of our needs at the same time. Don't forget the ultimate goal of life: to bring glory to His name, to point people to Jesus. Lord God, we want to represent you when we are long gone from this place. Your words spoken by God will still happen. My dad, the late Prophet Jacob Schroeder, spoke prophetic words that are still happening. God's word can't and won't fail. So don't stop speaking over your life because it's going to happen. Do you believe? Say yes: "Lord, I believe." And I will see the goodness of the Lord in the land of the living.

BREAKING OUT OF LIMITATIONS

Don't despise small beginnings. Nothing that God does in our lives is small. It's simply called small because it's just in seed form. It's in the process of being formed and developed. I am praying for three things for you: first, that you will pray; secondly, that you would have patience, understanding that it's going to take time to build what God has given you; and lastly, that you would be persistent, no matter what you face in the process of building. There is more—more to life than what you see, more understanding of what's happening in the world, and where we fit. He wants to tell you more, show you more, give you more. The Bible says not to be conformed to this world. Don't allow all of what's happening in the world to define who you are. Shifting your patterns and focus can change your life. Romans 12:2 talks about renewing your mind, changing the way you think to create a better life for yourself and a life that honors God. The world and society have patterns or ways that lead to a broken life. But God's way will always produce *all things new.* God is getting ready to change the way you see things.

Listen, through the lenses of God, it's finished. From the view of heaven, it's good. God just wants you to believe and trust Him. That's it. Seeing is not always believing. That's not how it works. We have to believe it before we see it. God says, "Just break out!" Imagine being in a jail cell with your hands and feet bound but the door is open. What does this mean? You have the ability to walk right out of the situation, but your hands and feet are bound. That's the part that God wants to address. He wants you free indeed.

Don't let your past speak louder than your future. If you notice when the leaves fall, they are dry and withered because they are no longer connected to their life source. Why are we still allowing things that are not connected to our destiny to speak louder than our destiny? God is healing us from the disappointment of the honeymoon stage dwindling or being over. Many of us get so excited when we begin things, and we put all of our energy into whatever we start... until the thrill is gone. Don't give up so soon, don't lose heart right in the building stage of whatever you're doing. Stay consistent and stay connected to God. Keep praying about the revamping and restructuring of the vision. The vision was given initially, yes, but some people stop seeking God for the rest and stay on the same flow without expansion. God says there is more. BE OPEN. Your vision is worth it, and the people that it will bless and encourage are worth it.

THE KEY TO RECEIVING IS GIVING

God has been repeatedly saying to me throughout this week, "The key to receiving is giving." The breakthrough you've been waiting for in your finances, debt, family, marriage, business, ministry, or any area is coming when you give. It's more blessed to give than to receive. The Bible says, "Give, and it shall be given unto you; pressed down, shaken together, and running over will God cause men to give unto you" (Luke 6:38). There are over 2,000 references in the Bible to the poor. When you give to the least, you're giving to God. According to Matthew 25:35-40, whatever you did for one of the least, you did for me. Psalm

41:1 says, "Blessed is the one who considers the poor! In the day of trouble, the Lord delivers him." Proverbs 14:21 says, "Whoever despises his neighbor is a sinner, but blessed is he who is generous to the poor."

Some of you may be saying, "I don't really have the money to give." But you may have time, resources, prayers, or whatever capacity you're able to give. Just give, and your cup will run over. You will be blown away by what's going to happen in your life before the end of this year. I am unapologetic when it comes to doing God's will. If my purpose offends you, I'm sorry, but I have to keep going.

You know what you're feeling right now—the friction of trying to move past your past responses, past failures, past mental challenges that you struggle with. Think of yourself trying to get past a small space. The Bible says, "Narrow is the way to God; broad is the way to destruction" (Matthew 7:14). So, this season may be tight for you. "I feel the friction, but I'm getting past it."

I know it's tempting to compromise who God says you are to gain the popularity of people. To get likes, it's tempting to rub elbows with the elite. God doesn't want you concerned about your name being known in the world. He wants you to rejoice that your name is written in the Book of Life. God wants us to live eternally with Him after it's all said and done. No pain, no sickness, no bills, and no trouble. Just goodness, worship, praise, eternity with our Father.

We have been rescued from sin and born into righteousness. Accept Jesus as your Savior and seal your ticket in heaven. What are you waiting for? If God is the one with the details of your life, there's no need to question how it's going to turn out. He knows the details, so stay close. I want to do what He says—it's that simple. Why would I try to live it on my own when I don't have to? That's the hard and long way. With His way comes peace, joy, freedom, and rest—just to name a few.

BEING READY FOR WHAT'S NEXT

You're trying to figure out if you're ready for what's next. You're praying for it, but have you prayed, "Lord, what do I need to do to get ready?" He will walk you through the process along the way. Being ready is not having everything you need to start; being ready is a mindset. Whenever a vision is conceived, it's done in the mind first. Before you do anything, it's a thought. This is why your mind has to be conditioned for what God wants for your life. What are you feeding your mind? What are you watching? Who are you listening to? These factors determine how you think, what you do, and who you become. Our minds have to be reprogrammed by God. He wants us to think like He thinks, and when we think differently, we see differently, we perceive differently, and then we move differently.

We can't make the same moves and get the same results. We have to do it God's way. How do you do this? Have you read about Him in the Bible? Is that really your daily bread? Is that what you feed on? Do you talk to Him? Have you spent time with Him? Do you know the people that you stay around? The most influential people are the ones that have the greatest influence on you. Many people are seeking to be great influencers in the world, and we try to model after people we see on TV who are deemed successful. But I want to tell you and introduce you to the most influential person in the entire world, and that's God. He created the people we're looking up to. When you shift your focus on things, you shift your life. Don't let your focus be on things that are temporary or fleeting; focus on the things that are eternal.

If you're wondering if God is real, take a moment and touch your arm and your face. You are living proof that He is real. There have been so many scientific explanations to try to explain how this world was framed and how we were created—the Big Bang theory, the evolution theory, and many more. But please tell me, how can you explain something supernatural happening without revelation? So you have scientists trying to figure out what God did by human knowledge. You can't explain something that you didn't do without knowledge from the one who did it. You can't explain the trees knowing when to grow, the leaves knowing when to fall off, the flowers knowing when to bloom. Babies knowing when to form and be birthed. The organs in your body know what to do—the blood flowing, your heart beating. *You are supernatural*, and God wants you to be born again. You were born naturally, but now you have to be born in the spiritual. And Jesus made that possible when He sacrificed His life for us to be free from sin and born into our new life with Christ, the Son of God. So stop trying to explain what

God is doing in your life to people without a revelation. God will reveal Himself to those who seek Him with all their heart.

You pray and release it in the earth, and as the Word says, "Write the vision, make it plain, and they that read it will run." Meaning they will understand. When you take the time to read something, this means you want to know more about the topic at hand. It's something you haven't seen before. Your vision is new. It will spark the interest of those who read it and cause them to be enlightened to start theirs. Please know that with God, we always win, and I know you're wondering how your life is going to pan out. Don't rush to try to make what God said happen. If God promised it, it will happen. We just have to stay in a posture of obedience to His will for our lives. God says, "If I'm with you and for you, and working through you, you can't lose." When your life is dedicated to God, change takes place. He's doing the change. Your appetite for the former things before accepting Christ decreases. I just know your character has to match where God called you to be before you get there. So don't rush the process. Let Him heal you and bring you to a level of maturity where you will be able to handle where He's taking you.

Come out of agreement with the belief that you will never get past where you are right now. You will get past it, through it, and rise above it. Everything is going up. You know how on the job, sometimes quarterly, you get evaluated to see if promotion is even in question. So be careful how you use your time. Are you building or tearing down? If you're tearing down, let it be something that needs to be done away with. What you do now will determine where you go later.

God wants to do and will do for you, but what will you do for Him? Will we forsake all and follow Jesus? We are praying and wanting God to answer all of our prayers. The key to getting answered prayers is to pray according to God's will for our lives because if it is His will, it's going to be answered. We should be grateful that God didn't give us what we wanted in the moment. We don't have to work for our blessing, but it's just like a parent who wants to give their children things, but they won't clean their home, they won't do their homework, yet they want things. God is our Father, and He purposed us to be here for a reason, so yes, there's a prerequisite to receiving the promises of God. If He was releasing the promises to you on Fifth Street and He said, "I need you to be on Fifth Street on December 19 at 5 PM," you wouldn't even know the location of where your blessings are because you're not communicating with God and you're not in a relationship with Him to hear His voice and know His instructions. He said, "If you love me, keep my commandments." When God saves us from the hold that our sinful nature has on us and brings us into freedom from it, our lives are changed forever. We no longer desire to live the same life as before.

There's nothing that God won't tell you to do that won't be beneficial to your life, your spouse, your family, and those you are praying for. So some of us are saying that we're waiting on God, but God is waiting on you to get in place. Some of us are simply out of position. You are one instruction away from receiving everything that God has for you. Turn on your spiritual navigation and wait for instructions from God.

THE TARGET OF GOD'S AFFECTION

God is coming after the area that screams louder than any other area. It's time to hit the target. It's time to be honest with God. What's bothering you? What's really going on? What triggers you? What is it that you hear that makes you shut down or go off? What makes you step out of character? It's that part that God wants. It's time to stop sweeping it under the rug. God is coming after the rejection, He's coming after the victim mentality. You are what you say you are. But you have to know the truth of the matter about your life. What are you? Who are you? Stop claiming what you are not and start proclaiming from the mountaintop who you are and that the life Christ died for is yours.

Punch out of hopelessness, punch out of despair, punch out of offense, punch out of depression, punch out of jealousy, and punch out of drug addiction. Speak over yourself: "I'm punching into prosperity, freedom, wholeness, favor. I'm punching into all God said about me." And when you do this, it dismantles all that garbage. I'm getting all that God has to offer!

Sometimes we try to figure out why. God needs to change your mindset so that He can change your life. *"I don't fit in because I was called to stand out."* Again, *"I don't fit in because I was called to stand out.."* Sometimes we try so hard to be accepted that we find ourselves compromising for the sake of pleasing man. So many people didn't reach their potential trying to stay on good terms with people they were not even called to impact. God will send you to unfamiliar territory, out of the norm, out of your comfort zone, to change the world we live in.

EMBRACING YOUR UNIQUE PURPOSE

You are different on purpose for a purpose. We look different and are wired differently, but we're sent here on earth for one purpose. Keep your eyes on God and what He specifically fashioned you to be. It may ruffle some feathers, but it's needed; it's necessary. You were born at the time you were supposed to be here, for this era. So, rise up and be who God called you to be! Your time is now!

GOD'S BAILOUT: BREAKING FREE FROM BONDAGE AND EMBRACING SALVATION

God says, "I'm bailing you out of the prison you've put yourself in because of life and the circumstances that have come your way. I also want to speak to the person who doesn't even realize they are in a prison." The bail has already been paid—it was the divine work of Jesus' sacrifice that bailed you out of the prison you are in today. God just wants you to receive your freedom through salvation. He wants to be Lord over your life so that you won't be bound by the foolishness that sometimes comes our way while we are here.

Bondage or slavery to strongholds in your life is not what God purposed for you. Psalm 62:8 says, "Trust in Him at all times, pour out your heart before Him; God is a refuge for us." He is your defender. He is everything you're trying to be by yourself, relying on your own strength. But He wants to take that load off your shoulders. You are not built to carry that stress. You were built to carry the glory of God— to be a vessel of His presence and a tool for His purposes in changing the world.

IT'S TIME TO CROSS OVER

Making a commitment to "crossing over" requires clear direction from the Word of God. This is a transitional moment for you, and God is redefining who you are and what you will be in the next season.

3 Keys to Crossing Over

To cross over successfully, you need to consider the following three keys:

1. *Leave the Past Behind:* You have to be willing to let go of the past and its baggage.
2. *Trust God's Instructions:* Trust God's plan and instructions, even when you don't fully understand them.
3. *Don't Fear the Unknown:* Don't be afraid of the unknown; instead, have faith that God is guiding you.

In Mark 4:35-41, Jesus told His disciples, "Let's go over to the other side." As they set sail, Jesus fell asleep, leaving the disciples to worry about the storm. But Jesus rebuked the wind and the storm, and they reached the other side safely. This story teaches us that God is always in control and that we need to trust His instructions and timing.

Whatever we do, we must do it for God's glory, not for our own purposes. We should not act to prove ourselves to others or gain their approval. Instead, we should focus on pleasing God and serving others. There will be two types of people in our lives: those who sincerely cheer for us and those who cheer for us to fail. But we must not let the opinions of others dictate our actions. We must focus on our purpose and let God guide us.

When Jesus was being crucified, He could have easily let His emotions get the better of Him. But instead, He focused on His purpose and prayed for His crucifiers, saying, "Forgive them, for they know not what they do." This teaches us not to waste time trying to please people but to focus on pleasing God and fulfilling our purpose. There are people out there who need what we have, and their lives can be changed by the purpose God has placed in us. Let's shift our focus from ourselves and onto God.

Crossing over is a significant step of faith that requires us to trust God's plan and timing. By leaving the past behind, trusting God's instructions, and not fearing the unknown, we can overcome any obstacle and fulfill our purpose. Remember, our actions should be motivated by a desire to please God and serve others, not by a desire to prove ourselves to others. Let's focus on our purpose and let God guide us as we cross over into a new season of life.

LETTING GOD RELEASE HIS PROMISES

Let Him clear out the clutter so that the treasure within can be revealed. Some of us have heard so much negativity and misinformation that when we finally hear the truth, we reject it. But God is saying, "Let me remove the junk so that the treasure can be seen." The Lord led me to Isaiah 60:11, which says, "Your gates will always stand open; they will never be shut, day or night, so that people may bring you the wealth of the nations—their kings led in triumphal procession." God is getting ready to release everything He has promised you. This is why it's essential to release all the things that have been weighing you down to Him. Place all of your gifts and talents on the altar so that God can do with them what He originally intended from the foundation of the world.

There is nothing that God will withhold from His children who walk uprightly before Him. But can He trust you with the abundance you're asking for? Will you handle the blessings wisely? Will you give Him the glory? Will you let your light shine so that others are drawn to Jesus? Heaven is where my promises lie; that's where I'm seated and where I receive my instructions on how to live my life here on earth through the Word of God.

Are you trying to determine the next step, what you need to do, or how to move forward? Pray, and God will release that direction to you. When you are in consistent communication with Him, He will provide what you need even before you ask. Don't you think He wants you to know? Of course, He does. The question is, would you act on it if you knew? Would you obey, or would you start doubting, coming up with reasons why you can't do what He has already created you to do?

He says, "Be holy, for I am holy." Righteousness is given to us through the blood of Jesus Christ. We can't earn what Christ died for; we simply have to receive it. John 3:3 says, "Unless a man is born again, he cannot see the Kingdom of God." Now is the time to live your victorious life God's way. And that is true freedom. Victory is based on the promises of God, not on the current circumstances. A victorious life isn't free from trouble, but God is there with us through it all, making it work for our good. So don't get sidetracked by what you see; stay focused and keep your eyes on what you know God has said.

> *"Do not lay up for yourselves treasures on earth, where moth and rust destroy and where thieves break in and steal; but lay up for yourselves treasures in heaven, where neither moth nor rust destroys and where thieves do not break in and steal."*
>
> — MATTHEW 6:19-21

God told me to tell you, whether it's morning, evening, or whenever you hear this, that this time it's going to happen. God is bringing you from the back to the front. That can mean many things to different people, but it's a shift in position that He has orchestrated. You may have thought you were ready when you prayed about it, but God knew you had some lessons to learn first.

It's not just about receiving what God promised; it's about being positioned to walk in that promise, to steward it well, and to teach others how to do the same. Sometimes, we focus so much on obtaining the promise that we forget why God positioned us in the first place—to show others what God looks like on earth through His children who carry His DNA.

We must let Him be Lord over our lives by giving Him total access and completely surrendering our will. His plan works every time; ours may not follow through because it is temporary. I want the eternal stability and assurance that my life will be successful, don't you? Trust in this: "God will make good on His investment in me."

ALIGNING WITH GOD'S WILL

God's will is good for us—yes, His plan is perfect. Romans 12:2 says, "Do not conform any longer to the pattern of this world, but be transformed by the renewing of your mind. Then you will be able to test and approve what God's will is—his good, pleasing, and perfect will."

So, let go of the patterns of the world—the cheating, the lying, and the shortcuts that seem necessary to get ahead. God is our fast tracker. He's the one who seals the deals, brings order, removes people and things that are not in our best interest, and convicts us in love when we're straddling the fence, unsure if we want to live the separated, consecrated life that Jesus died to give us.

When your mind is transformed, you no longer desire to flow according to the world's standards because that is what God saves us from. We are now flowing in God's perfect will because we have the mind of Christ. We are able to test and prove because of this. Not every door of opportunity is from God. We cannot be deceived by anything the kingdom of darkness tries to throw our way because Jesus is the light, and we are heirs with God, joint heirs with Jesus Christ. We walk in the light. So, don't conform—be transformed!

Today, I want to remind you: don't forget to live. Sometimes, we can be so caught up in the "what ifs" and the "what nots" that we forget to live in the moment. What are you supposed to be doing right now? Don't get overwhelmed by the vision just because your present situation doesn't match what God said. What you see right now is not the determining factor that will create the vision that God showed you. He already has it all worked out. The question is, do you trust God?

What you do now will determine whether you reach that vision and carry it out. Don't allow anxiety, worry, stress, people, or circumstances to stop you from dreaming. If God showed it to you, that means He's going to do it. As a matter of fact, it's already done. That means He wants it to happen for you. That means nothing in your life right now can stop that from happening.

So, listen to the instructions He's telling you to do right now. Live in the now so that you can get to your future. Many of you are in a transitional moment in your life where it is vitally important that you listen to every instruction that God gives you. You're getting ready to walk into a new, territorial position of authority that is necessary for your growth. In this new place, you will become knowledgeable of who you are and what God has called you to be, and it's going to make the enemy afraid.

You may not understand why God is pulling you away from some things. You won't be accepted everywhere, and there are things that you won't feel comfortable about anymore. But you have to know that your steps are ordered by God. God is exposing things—things that you needed to see before you made your final decision. For some, this changed your decision; for others, your decision will remain the same, but God wanted to make you aware. You have been exposed.

There is a recalibrating happening in the spirit—carefully assess, set, and adjust the things in your life that are out of sync with God's original plan. The set order of things that worked in the previous season may no longer work, but God says, "For where you're going, I need to recalibrate you. I need to reset you. I need to adjust your mind, align your heart posture, and heal all of those broken places."

Some things that happened in your life will no longer scar you. They will no longer stop or hinder you from moving forward into your predestined life. You have to be determined, through and by the power of God, through the redeeming power of salvation given to us through the blood of Jesus shed on the cross. It is our divine inheritance to receive healing and be whole and live out the life that God planned.

If there is anything in your life hindering that from happening, it has illegal access in your life, and you have the power to command it to go so that you can fulfill your destiny. Be determined to let nothing get in the way. Romans 8:38-39 says, "For I am persuaded, that neither death, nor life, nor angels, nor principalities, nor powers, nor things present, nor things to come, nor height, nor depth, nor any other creature shall be able to separate us from the love of God which is in Christ Jesus our Lord."

THE CLOSING

I enter into my heavenly place, a place of promise, limitless blessings, limitless power, and limitless authority in Christ Jesus. I exit the outer court of carnality and receive the Spirit of the living God in all of Your glory and majesty within my being. I call forth the heavenly realm to come into this earthly space, so that this space will give way to the glory of God. Let this earthly realm experience the heavenly host and the presence of the Almighty God in a way that has never been seen before in humanity.

God says, "I am going to show you My glory and great manifestations that cannot be fully described or articulated. You cannot even begin to understand in your human mind what I am gathering together, putting together, and orchestrating to happen in this dispensation, if you would only let go of yourself. If you would only take the attention off of yourself, you will see Me take over your life completely. Everything in your life must change so that I can be Lord, so that I can be Master, so that I can be King over your mind, over your actions, over your entire life.

You have not seen anything yet; wait until I show you what you have been missing. Wait until I show you what happens when you come up to the mountain of the Lord, when you enter into a realm that you've never seen before. When you stop trying to make it happen yourself, you will understand that this is My doing, and it is marvelous in your eyes. You will be awed by what you're getting ready to see; you will be amazed. And what you have been missing, which has been trying to enter into your life, was hindered by too many things in the way. I could not come in My pureness because of confusion and entanglement with the things of this world. There was a web of confusion from the outer court to the inner court that was in the way, and you were entangled in this web. But now you see the web of confusion that's around you. You see what has been trying to hold you back in this place of complacency.

Now that the web is clear, you can walk into the new thing that you have been feeling and sensing. The time is now; it's here. You are elevated; you are getting ready to go higher than you have ever been before because you are in another realm. You are not in the same place;

you cannot be around the same people. In fact, those people are not going to want to be around you because you are in another sphere in the spiritual realm that no one around you who is not in the same sphere will understand. You're going to irritate people who refuse to come up; you're going to become an enemy to those who refuse to ascend higher than where they have been.

So, I need you to stay in a place of brokenness, stay humble before Me, listen to My every instruction, and follow through on every directive. When you do that, you will see progression in your life and in every area. Follow everything that I say—don't move until I give you instruction."

INTERACTIVE ACTIVITY (PART 1)

Multiple Choice Fill-in-the-Blank

1. According to the Oxford language dictionary, induction refers to the action or process of _____ someone to a particular position or organization.

    a) creating
    b) introducing
    c) transforming
    d) redeeming

2. According to 2 Corinthians 3:18, we are being transformed into the same image from glory to glory as we _____ the Lord.

    a) see
    b) behold
    c) hear
    d) know

3. According to 1 John 3:2, we will be like Christ when He appears, because we will _____ Him as He is.

    a) see
    b) hear
    c) know
    d) understand

4. According to the text, God gave us a _____ that creates sound.

    a) voice
    b) word
    c) language

d) spirit

5. According to the text, words have the power to _____ and destroy.

    a) create
    b) destroy
    c) build
    d) uplift

INTERACTIVE ACTIVITY (PART 2)

Short Answer Questions

1. How did you receive your identity?

_____
_____
_____
_____
_____
_____
_____
_____

2. What does it mean to be made alive in Christ?

_____
_____
_____
_____
_____
_____
_____
_____

3. What is the importance of reading and declaring scriptures daily?

_____

_____

_____

_____

_____

_____

_____

_____

4. What does it mean to be sanctified saints?

_____

_____

_____

_____

_____

_____

_____

_____

5. How can we use our words to create and uplift?

_____

_____

_____

_____

_____

_____

_____

_____

Appendix

This section provides the answer key for the interactive activities found in each chapter. Use it as a guide to reinforce your understanding and ensure you're on the right track as you work through the material.

* * *

Chapter 3: Bound to Break
— Part 2 —

Multiple Choice:
1. b) The maximum amount that something can hold
2. a) Noah
3. b) To love our enemies
4. a) That our resources can be multiplied if we have faith
5. b) To forgive without any conditions
6. b) Job
7. a) Our bodies are limited and frail
8. c) We should use our talents to serve and multiply them
9. b) Peter
10. b) Unlimited and unconditional

11. e) All of the above

Chapter 4: When I Broke, I Healed

Fill-in-the-Blank:
1. broken / new
2. relief / growth
3. Stagnation / underdevelopment / grace
4. fortification / sense
5. normal / healing
6. broken / broken
7. produces / character / character
8. reservations / new
9. trauma
10. healed

Chapter 6: Strategies for War
— Part 1 —

Fill-in-the-Blank:
1. pray
2. problems
3. eternal
4. revelation
5. voice

Multiple Choice:
1. b) To identify the root cause
2. c) Receiving a revelation of who God is and our identity in Him

— Part 2 —

Fill-in-the-Blank:
1. community
2. restoration
3. spiritual

4. royal

Multiple Choice Questions:
1. b) It symbolizes divine approval and empowerment
2. b) Knowing God intimately
3. a) To communicate with God

Chapter 7: The Induction of the New You
— Part 1 —

Multiple Choice Fill-in-the-Blank:
1. b) introducing
2. b) behold
3. a) see
4. a) voice
5. a) create

BIBLIOGRAPHY

Bandler, Dr., and Dr. Grinder. *The Psychology of the Subconscious Mind*. Real People Press, 2020.

Barrett, David P. *The Encyclopedia of Biblical Names and Meanings*. Print.

Bible. New International Version. Grand Rapids, MI: Zondervan, 2011.

Bible. Romans 9:27-29. Translated by [translator], OnePassion Ministries, April 25, 2019.

"Broken Soul Overview." Operation Light Force, 2023.

Chloe, M. "What Is in Your Alabaster Box? Lay Your Dreams at God's Feet." *Letters to Women Podcast,* August 30, 2012, https://letterstowomenpodcast.com/blog/2012/08/30/428.

Cornell University. "New Study Reveals Where Memory Fragments are Stored." *Newsroom,* Cornell University, January 27, 2022, https://news.weill.cornell.edu/news/.

Davis, Nathan. "Ezra and the Returnees: Restoring the Laws and Customs of Israel." Journal of Old Testament Studies, vol. 25, no. 4, 2020, pp. 112-129.

Diodorus Siculus. *Bibliotheca Historica*. 50-30 BCE. Book 1, Chapter 9.

Eternal Wall of Answered Prayer. "Walls in Scripture." *Eternal Wall of Answered Prayer,* https://www.eternalwall.org.uk/walls-in-scripture/.

"Eagle Symbolism." *Native Languages.org,* 2020, https://www.nativelanguages.org/eagle-symbolism/.

"Eagle Symbolism and Meaning." *A-Z Animals,* 2020, https://a-z-animals.com/animal-category/eagle-symbolism-and-meaning/.

"Eagle Symbolism in Christianity." *Catholic Online,* 2020, https://www.catholic.org/prayer/saints/a-z/eagle-symbolism-in-christianity.php.

Erdoes, Richard. *The Tales of the Grandfathers*. Print.

Fowler, Alastair. *The Oxford Dictionary of Christian Quotations*. Print.

Gesenius. *The Hebrew Dictionary*. Print.

Grudem, Wayne A. *Christian Ethics: An Introduction to Biblical Ethics*. InterVarsity Press, 2018.

Hastings, James. *Dictionary of the Bible*. Vol. 1. New York: Charles Scribner's Sons, 1909, p. 593.

Hawkins, Dr. David R. *The Subconscious Mind: A Guide to Unlocking the Power of Your Hidden Mind*. Hay House, Inc., 2020.

Homer's Iliad. Greek and Roman mythology texts.

Jackson, S. G. *The New Testament Greek-English Dictionary*. Boston: Crocker & Brewster, 1836.

Johnson, Mark. "The Promise of Restoration: A Study of the Rebuilding of Jerusalem." Jerusalem Studies, vol. 4, no. 2, 2018, pp. 45-62.

Josephus Flavius. *Antiquities of the Jews*. 93-100 AD. Book 12, Chapter 6, Section 4.

Jung, Carl. *The Symbolism of Animals*. Print.

Kapoor, Avinash, et al. "Circadian Rhythms and Sleep." *Journal of Sleep Research,* vol. 26, no. 2, 2017, pp. 131-141, doi: 10.1111/jsr.12463.

Keener, Craig S. *The IVP Bible Background Commentary: New Testament*. InterVarsity Press, 1993.

King, Matt, and Christopher Watson. "Title of the Article." University of Tasmania, August 5, 2022, 12:10 a.m. EDT.

Lewis, Lee. "Contributing Factors to a Crushed Spirit According to Proverbs." September 27, 2023.

McKnight, Scot. *The King Jesus Gospel: The Original Good News Revisited*. Zondervan, 2011.

Merriam-Webster Dictionary, s.v. "underdevelopment," https://www.merriam-webster.com/dictionary/underdevelopment.

Murphy, Joseph. *The Power of the Subconscious Mind*. Prentice Hall Press, 2020.

National Institute of General Medical Sciences, National Institutes of Health. "The Brain's Activity Patterns Are Regulated by an Internal Clock." *NIGMS*, 2020,

https://www.nigms.nih.gov/education/brain-basics/brain-basics-overview/Pages/
default.aspx.

National Sleep Foundation. "Brain Activity and Sleep." *Sleep Foundation,* 2020, https://
www.sleepfoundation.org/sleep-topics/brain-activity-and-sleep.

New American Bible, Confraternity of Christian Doctrine, 1987, p. 1831.

Oxford Dictionary of First Names, edited by Patrick Hanks and Flavia Hodges. Oxford
University Press, 2006, p. 282.

Oxford English Dictionary, s.v. "dysfunctionalism," https://en.oxforddictionaries.com/
definition/dysfunctionalism.

Smith, Rachel. "Zerubbabel and the Rebuilding of the Temple: A Leader's Journey of
Faith." Biblical Leadership Quarterly, vol. 12, no. 3, 2019, pp. 18-27.

Talmud. Bava Batra 10b.

Thompson, David. "The Spiritual Walls of Jerusalem: Repentance, Prayer, and Obedience
in the Rebuilding Process." Sacred Scriptures Review, vol. 17, no. 2, 2022, pp. 77-90.

Townsend, Sarah. "Making 'Disruption' a Positive Word." *Iipay,* February 27, 2020,
https://www.iipay.com/making-disruption-a-positive-word/.

Underwood, Jolene. "Why You Can Be Sure 'the Lord Is Close to the Brokenhearted'
(Psalm 34:18)." Updated August 27, 2020.

University of Michigan Health. "Malunion Fractures." University of Michigan Health,
July 14, 2022, https://www.uofmhealth.org/cmc.

White, Sarah. "Nehemiah: The Cupbearer Called to Rebuild." Faith and Leadership
Journal, vol. 8, no. 1, 2021, pp. 55-68.

ACKNOWLEDGMENTS

As I reflect on the journey of writing this book, I am deeply aware that I did not walk this path alone. Many individuals and communities have provided support, encouragement, and inspiration, all of which have been instrumental in bringing my vision to life.

First and foremost, I want to express my heartfelt gratitude to my parents, the late *Prophet Jacob Schroeder* and *Missionary Exemea Schroeder*: Your faith, love, and unwavering dedication to God laid the foundation upon which my life is built. Your teachings continue to guide me, and their memory inspires me every day.

I also extend my thanks to my two older brothers, *Eric Schroeder* and *Antonio Schroeder*: Your steadfast support throughout this journey. Each of you has contributed to my understanding of faith and family in unique ways, and I am grateful for the shared experiences that have enriched my life.

To my loving son, *Joshua Evans:* I am so proud of you. Your ambition, brilliance, and self-sufficiency as a visionary at such a young age are remarkable. You are already the author of four books, a game developer, and an upcoming business owner— all of this starting at the age of ten (10) and now continuing at fifteen (15). I thank God for the special gift that you are, and I promise to continue building a strong foundation in Christ, as led by the Holy Spirit, so that you can continue to be a light of God in the world.

To my mentors and spiritual leaders, *Archbishop Ralph Dennis & Lady Deborah Dennis, Bishop Gregory Dennis & Pastor Tonya Dennis*, I am deeply thankful for your guidance and wisdom. Your insights have helped shape my understanding during pivotal moments in my life and in my role within it. I am especially grateful for the encouragement you offered when I needed it most.

I am also thankful for the *prophetic voices* in my life that continue to encourage and strengthen me on this journey. You know who you are; you are loved and appreciated.

Thank you, *Bishop Damien Sneed,* for writing the song "Broken to Minister." From the very first time I heard it, the song resonated deeply within my spirit and ministered to my soul. Listening to it throughout the writing process served as a powerful reminder that my brokenness is purposeful and has prepared me—and will continue to prepare me—for ministry.

A special thanks to all my *friends and ministry partners* who have provided support, prayers, and laughter, and who have helped me bear my cross. Your belief in my writing has encouraged me to step out of my comfort zone and share my truth.

To my editor, *Nicole Queen*, thank you for being a great supporter and destiny pusher. You have ensured that I poured out all that God has given me in my writings, and you have been the catalyst that made the finished product immaculate. Thank you also to your company, Vision Publishing, and to all the fellow authors who took the time to read my drafts and provide feedback. Your constructive criticism and encouragement have strengthened my work, and for that, I am truly thankful.

Lastly, but certainly not least, I extend my deepest gratitude to *God*— my Father, my friend, my confidant, my healer, my deliverer, my sustainer, my peace, my joy, my everything. Without

You, this book could never have been written. This book is the expression of the finger of God. The evidence of being tried in the fire is truly reflected in it, with You walking alongside me and the vision of me coming out as pure gold. May I continue to stay on the Potter's wheel, embracing the "brokenness" for the rest of my earthly days. Abba, You are my inspiration, and Your presence has illuminated my path. It is my prayer that this book reflects Your love and grace.

Thank you to everyone who has played a part in this endeavor. Your contributions— both big and small— have made this journey not only possible but deeply fulfilling.

ABOUT THE AUTHOR

Crystal Love, a native of Baltimore, is a dedicated mother, Elder, and Prophet within the Christian community. She committed her life to the Lord in 1997 at the age of 17 and was called to ministry at 20. With 25 years of ministry experience, Crystal currently serves as an Elder at Kingdom Worship Center in Baltimore, MD, under the leadership of Bishop Gregory Dennis and Pastor Tonya Dennis.

Passionate about community service, Crystal volunteers in homeless shelters, teaches at women's transitional homes, engages in outreach and evangelism, and hosts empowerment events aimed at uplifting and encouraging individuals to walk in their God-given callings. In 2011, she founded Holistic Ministries, focusing on addressing the comprehensive needs of individuals—spiritual, emotional, social, and physical. Holistic Ministries, Inc. is a parachurch affiliate of Kingdom Fellowship Covenant Ministries, Inc., under the leadership of her spiritual father, Archbishop Ralph Dennis.

An author of several books that promote healing and wholeness, Crystal holds a Bachelor's degree in Pastoral Counseling, equipping her to help others recover through the power of the Holy Spirit. She is currently pursuing a Bachelor of Science degree with a focus on Religion and Christian Leadership & Ministries. Her ministry reflects her deep commitment to helping individuals discover their purpose in Jesus Christ and further expand the Kingdom of God.

"When Jesus saw him lie, and knew that he had been now a long time in that case, he saith unto him, Wilt thou be made whole?"

— JOHN 5:6

Be sure to purchase your copy of the "Broken to Build" Bible Study Curriculum & 30-Day Devotional

For more books and updates:

🌐 crystallove-theauthor.com
✉ hello@crystallove-theauthor.com
f facebook.com/crystal_love
🐦 twitter.com/crystalcauthor
📷 instagram.com/holisticministrieslove

Scan below to listen to the "Broken to Build" Pronouncement

For Access
Use Password: Listen

www.ingramcontent.com/pod-product-compliance
Lightning Source LLC
Chambersburg PA
CBHW070921120626
46546CB00001B/350